T0132179

The Pain Journal

BOB FLANAGAN

The Pain Journal
BOB FLANAGAN

Semiotext(e) / Smart Art Press

A note on production: The conditions under which Bob Flanagan
typed these journal entries are illustrated not only in the content of
the entries, but also in their typographical errors and idiosyncracies,
most of which have intentionally been left intact.

Smart Art Press Volume VII, number 69.
ISBN: 978-1-58435-002-6

Semiotext(e) Native Agents Series
www.semiotexte.org

Distributed by The MIT Press, Cambridge, Massachusetts, and
London, England

The MIT Press is pleased to keep this title available in print by manu-
facturing single copies, on demand, via digital printing technology.

When Bob Flanagan began The Pain Journal on November 22, 1994, he only had another 408 days to live. He knew this, and he didn't. The exact Hour of His Death is a subject he returns repeatedly to in the journal, with mordant wit, though certainly there are others: the real or imagined betrayal by friends and associates in the art and literary world; the exhilaration and futility of producing and exhibiting art works and the furious contradiction between his lust for physical pain, as a masochist and his rage at the involuntary pain that he was now subject to. All these thoughts arise in tandem with the banal minutae, also faithfully recorded, of the daily life of someone who is sick and dying. The Pain Journal reflects an extraordinary, courageous life, but it's just as much about the ordinariness of death itself.

Bob Flanagan was born with Cystic Fibrosis in 1952. The disease, first named and "discovered" in the mid-50s, killed most people of his generation during childhood. In his 20s, Flanagan did not expect to live beyond his early 30s. At the beginning of The Pain Journal, he has just turned 42. Cystic Fibrosis is a genetic disorder which kills a person slowly through the body's over-production of abnormally thick mucous lodging in the lungs which becomes a host for bacterial infections. Lack of sufficient oxygen causes depletion in the blood and brain (hence the excruciating headaches) and ultimately, the person drowns in his own secretions. And so The Pain Journal chronicles Bob's final year in which he is the subject of a bricolage of medical interventions aimed at alleviating the disease's symptoms while the disease itself, untreated and ultimately untreatable, gathers steam.

Flanagan began to document his co-existence with the disease in the mid-80s in his works with his wife and collaborator Sheree Rose. When they met in 1980, he was a poet—part of a group of younger writers including Amy Gerstler, Dennis Cooper, Benjamin Weissman and Jack Skelly—who found each other at the LA literary center, Beyond Baroque and formed an influential and supportive gang. He was also (child of two Irish Catholics) a masochist, a fact which he immediately announced to Sheree Rose, who at that time was, as Dennis Cooper wrote in Artforum, "a housewife turned punk scenester with a master's degree in psychology" with no experience with s/m. Rose quickly rose to it ... but while Bob told her that his greatest dream was to live chained up inside the basement of her Westwood home, Rose had other plans. Their relationship was very public—as Cooper recalled, "Bob was an exhibitionist, and Sheree loved to shock people ... It wasn't unusual to drop by and find the place full of writers, artists, and people from the s/m community, all flying on acid and/or speed, Bob naked and happily enacting orders from the leather-clad Sheree." So it wasn't a great leap when the two, at Sheree's prodding, mounted an extraordinary photo-collage, vignettes from their s/m play called The Wall of Pain, at a Beyond Baroque show of "Writers Who Make Art" in 1982. Together, they continued to make art works, installations and video's from their life together—s/m acts which were often staged against hospital beds and oxygen tanks, the paraphernalia of Bob's continued medical-maintenance regime, culminating in the production of Visiting Hours, a show which filled the Santa Monica Museum and rocked the art world in 1992.

The last year of Bob's life, 1995, finds the two in a mid-career flurry of traveling shows and interviews and panels, which he finds it increasingly difficult to do. He and Rose are collaborating with the filmmaker Kirby Dick on a documentary film about Bob's life, which would eventually be completed as Sick: The Life and Death of Bob Flanagan Supermasochist and go on to win the Special Grand Prize at Sundance in 1997. That summer, he drags himself out of his hospital bed to appear one last time at a summer camp for kids with Cystic Fibrosis, where he had been a counselor and director for 17 years. It is a generous and triumphant performance that is documented in the film. By 1995, he had become notorious for the ingenious uses for his body he and Sheree have devised. But meanwhile, during the insomniac small hours of the morning, while the TV drones and Sheree snores, he agonizes about his body's disappearance. Cystic fibrosis, like other lung diseases, causes a slow wasting. The only thing that he sees left of it most nights is his penis, and he worries constantly about how and whether he could use it.

While he became best-known for his multi-media works with Sheree Rose, Flanagan was essentially a writer, and it's no coincidence that he would choose The Pain Journal to be his final work. It is, perhaps, his bravest action: because while everyone might long for the "good death," one which is absent of recrimination and regret, death is a wild card, and a person's death does not necessarily have much to do with the person that we knew. Throughout the year, his paranoid ruminations of betrayal are inseparable from his cogent thoughts about his work and life and his unwavering devotion to Rose and other friends. Extreme pain does not afford the best perspective. For its truthfulness alone, The Pain Journal is a great literary work and document. As Flanagan's friend, the critic Deborah Drier, has said, "it is completely transparent, an essence of what he was going through."

—Chris Kraus

12/27/94 We are in NY. Gramercy Park Hotel. Bed. Forget what time it is—I mean who cares? Sheree's sleeping. Scott's sleeping. It's been an awful Christmas and an even worse birthday. My parents cramped, depressing apartment. No John. No kids. Me, my whiny, wheezy, grumbling self, scaring everyone out of their minds, acting like I'm going to die any moment. Still depressed now. I just want to die—I meant to write "cry" and I wrote "die." Tomorrow's the museum's B'day party. I'm anxious about it. Just want to be left alone, but I don't want to be alone. I don't want to be nice to anybody. Can't stand anyone. Hate myself. Just want to be home.

12/28/94 Birthday party over—thank God. Success, from the look of it. People. Nice presents. But me? Where the hell was I? People were impressed by me on the nails—but I wasn't *really* on the nails—not all of me—Two chicken shit to let go. "Couldn't breathe," my idiot's lament. Terrified at the sight of Sheree slicing the big marzipan penis on my stomach—afraid she'll go too far—accidents, afraid of accidents, so I can't get *into* anything. I'm always on the peripheral. I'm always terrified, exhausted, annoyed, pissed, anxious, nervous, impatient, just out of it—period, out of the loop, out of my mind, running out of time.

12/29/94 Everybody's out. I'm in. Everybody is Scott, Sheree and her friend, Jake (female). Not so depressed today, but getting around is tough. Chest hurts. Can't breathe. Blah blah blah. Interview by two Spanish guys and *USA Today*. Who am I that they should value my opinion on anything? What am I? I'm so afraid of being stupid.

12/30/94 Long day breathing badly and being scared about it. Thoughts of going home early. Thoughts of getting chest x-ray (is it a collapsed lung?). I increased my prednisone and that seemed to boost me a bit. Last day of VH tomorrow. New Year's Eve. Don't want to go out anywhere tomorrow night.

12/31/94 Happy New Year. Visiting Hours are over. Blab. Mitch Corber—pest from the past. Sheree—yes I love her—but in her normal state, not when she's stoned, and she's been stoned a lot this week, thanks to Scott. I don't relate. I wish I could, and I wish she would stop and just be herself, the one I get along with, the real one I love. But no such luck. She's out now, with Julia and Shelly, desperately searching for a good time, never giving up, never giving in, after a nice dinner (what the fuck is nice?). It was tense for me—too much talk about Bob Bob Bob Sheree Sheree Sheree art art art. Scott Kirby and Laura were there also, but mostly Sheree. "Do you want to hear my idea about Germany?" No! Please not now, but she's off, and she's drunk, and etc. But I do love her. Am I just saying that to wrap this thing up nicely? Bob—Mr. Nice Guy.

1/1/95 Of course the blow up. Slow, sleepy day. Wake up from a nap in the afternoon. Sheree, Scott, Kirby in the living room, stoned. Sheree bitching about her life, as usual. I toss her a Paxil. Join them. Laughs. Joking about tv and stuff and Shelly who turned out to be a shit last night. Suddenly Sheree gets Shelly's manuscript and says she's going to burn it, or goes to burn it and I say no, the sprinklers, too dangerous. Kirby and Scott agree. Kirby video taping. Suddenly Sheree gets up and comes back with the big candle (the one I got for my b'day) and a bowl—I guess for the ashes—and I flipped, grabbed the candle and threw it across the room, where it broke. "So what, it's *my* candle," I say. But that's it. Of course *I'm* the *monster*, I'm wrong. It's been cool from her ever since.

1/2/95 Bad stomach most of the day. Sheree out with Scott. Kirby out. Interviewed by Kathe Burkhardt for Kirby. Sheree, Scott, Kirby, Kathe stoned, drunk, loud, obnoxious (Sheree, anyway). Dinner at City Crab. The Piss Twins show up. Come back and they do a little show in the bedroom. But it's all too loud (Sheree) and everyone's too out of it for me. "$80 for a bottle of wine! Are you nuts?" "Oh, $18. That's different." Kathe asks us on tape when was the last time we fucked? We couldn't remember.

1/3/95 Took down the alphabet block wall with Scott, but even though he did the work I still couldn't breathe. Saw myself on the computer internet. "Pussy" letter on my e-mail. Dinner with Scott, Kirby, Laura, and Sheree. Calmer today. Nasty finger fuck, cunt lick, ass lick last night cause she begged me after those piss lesbians got her all hot. I didn't want to give her the time of day. I was just so pissed at her because I was tired of seeing her pissed/ wasted/ drunk/ loud. Felt like George Saunders. Cold. Sadistic. Superior. Mean. But I gave in cause I knew there would be hell to pay if I didn't. I knew how bad I'd feel afterwards. I knew how wrong I was.

1/4/95 Another dinner another night of people. If Sheree says "the internet" one more time I'm going to wish her into a corn field. Everything taken down at the museum it's a great feeling I'm ready to go home tomorrow will I be as out of breath there? Will Sheree get morose and miserable being back with nothing to do? Well, I have lots to do—my life, whatever it is.

1/5/95 Home home home. I know Sheree's not so thrilled. She's in bed sleeping now because she's got to be up for work tomorrow—but I'm glad to be home, even though it's a big mess and there's no food or milk and I don't really know what to do with myself other than sit here on the couch and doze off as I stare at the tv. Not ready for bed, but exhausted just the same. Flight was fine. Anti-anxiety pills. Kirby picked us up, camera in hand. When we get home I get a frantic call from Mom and Dad— TWA in Kansas called *them* wondering where *I* was. They said they had my oxygen waiting and I never got on the plane in New York. So of course they panicked and tried to reach us, called the hotel, called the car service—when all the time I was asleep on the plane. Nutty. But here I am. Nothing to say. Lots to do. Am I really in as bad shape as I felt much of the time away? I can't tell. Too relaxed.

1/6/95 Wake up early morning yelling at Sheree before she leaves for work because I get tired of her moaning and groaning about how bad she has it and how I wasn't able to do very much in New York. She's insatiable. Yelling seemed to help. She's been real good to me ever since, although I physically just don't have it. Made Debbie cry telling her how worried I am about getting worse and slipping away. Exaggeration? Problem is I don't know. Just don't know.

1/7/95 I'm a boring person who's dying. Feel dead. Wish I was but don't want to be. Want to be doing work. New work. It's time. All Sheree can think about is going going going. As far removed from work as you can get. But I was mad this morning because we're involved in some goofy show at Cal Arts and *we* have to supply the equipment and *we* have to deliver it. Life's too hard already to have to add more bullshit for little money and no prestige. And while I'm dwelling on death—Preston, 23 year old from cystic fibrosis camp, died a couple of days ago. Funeral tomorrow but I'm not going to go. Should have called him, but what would I have done, wished him luck?

1/8/95 Horrible stomach aches and nausea. Heavy little shits. Should I start taking *Wellbutrin?* Don't know. Am I sick or crazy? Short of breath everywhere I go. Making like I'm dying. Am I exaggerating? Why would I? Who would I be trying to impress? Drove Sheree out to Cal Arts with the fucking video projector today. Heavy rain. I like driving. It's the only time I can go from here to there and not feel completely wasted.

1/9/95   Cold in here. "Here" is the hospital again. Again I got tired and scared about not being able to breathe. What's the deal? I feel OK now, but—here's the guy to fix the cooler. A few minutes, he says. I keep thinking I'm dying, I'm dying, but I'm not, I'm not—not yet.

1/10/95   Don't write much in the hospital cause nothing happens and there's certainly nothing in my head. Tv tv tv. Low sat when I walk. At least I know I'm not crazy. But what's wrong with me? Cf, you jerk.

1/11/95   Almost forgot. It's real late. Slept and woke up. Watching *The Conversation* on tv. Never saw it before. Should go back to sleep. Gotta watch my health, you know. By the way— still in the hospital (where else?). Kind of depressed. All this time thinking I'm going to die—am I just talking myself into a frenzy of phlegm and fatigue? Maybe I'm getting better. Maybe I'm not. Now they say I should exercise. Exercise/Wheelchair. Exercise/Wheelchair. Hard to know what to do or who I am in it all.

1/12/95   Almost slipped off without writing. Have to do a little. Zone out when I'm in the hospital. All day working up a sweat just trying to breathe. Started physical therapy but the little bit of stretching she had me doing was tough. But everyone says I look good. Just feel like shit. Here's the nurse for drugs. Sheree called. *Autopsy* opening at Cal Arts group show. Everybody loves it and us and me, although it's getting harder to understand why.

1/13/95   Don't want to give it up to write anything. Don't have anything. Depressed. Taking big red Wellbutrin pills but still depressed. My shrink, Dr. Obler gone for two weeks. Can't get myself together. Stuck here in the hospital bed again. Too much. Now Boston U wants to exhibit our piece *Visiting Hours*. But it won't include me, just the stuff. "You know, and stuff." That's what Mom says: "You know, and stuff." No stuff here. And I don't know.

1/14/95   Mom and Dad's 45th anniversary—I made the call—no I didn't—they called me cause I'm the sick one in the hospital. Their sick child. Their dying boy. I keep having these flashes of anxiety where I feel I'm under some sort of weight or under water and I want to run but I can't get out. Sweating like crazy too. Sheree's out with Jake tonight. Marnie's party. I'm actually having sexual thoughts—some stirrings. Even masturbated in broad daylight, sitting right here in my hospital bed with a hard-on under my gown while he nurse brought me my dinner tray. "You got everything?" she asks. "Yes," I say. And I don't even lose my hard-on. Coming is always a let down, but at least I can do it— still alive.

1/15/95   The old *Perry Mason* show used to be so depressing when it came on, but now it's almost comforting. You get your comforts where you can these days here in the hospital. Life goes on and so does this depression. When my mother calls and tells me I sound like I'm getting better I tell her no, not really, not yet. I'm almost rude to her about it. No I'm not. I'm not better. I'm not ready to be better, so stop making me better already. And of course I spend the whole day feeling guilty abut it, how I almost cut her off because she was feeling good that I might be feeling better. I'll make it up to her—tomorrow I *will* be better, even though I just now spit up a big wad of blood—I'll still be better, just you wait and see.

1/16/95   I ask for Vicodin and then I put an alligator clip on my left nipple. It's all drugs. Thanks to the Wellbutrin (the lack of Paxil) I'm getting hard-ons again, and renewed fantasies of self torture. Want to be beaten by Sheree—someday I'll tell her. See what happens at home—Wednesday probably.

1/17/95 Tim's birthday. Anniversary of last year's quake. Day of new major quake in Japan. 2,000 killed. Thousands trapped. Scaring the hell out of myself watching this shit. Sheree wants to keep me locked in the cage at night when I get home, but I'm claustrophobic already, imagining myself trapped in the cage in a major quake, unable to find the key, Sheree lost, me screaming for help, out of oxygen. Short of breath already. But then, even without the cage, what's the difference—house, apartment—big cages without bars or sex appeal. I still can't breathe. Going home tomorrow. Home to lots of beatings—I hope.

1/18/95 Home. Buttplug up my ass. IV running through my chest. Sheree asleep downstairs. And I can sleep with her when I'm done, not in the cage like she said. I'm glad—sleeping in the cage would be hard after more than a week in bed without her, and it's so cold here. Yes, I get incredibly excited at the thought of her being cruel to me—endless hard-ons—but I love the reality of her being nice to me. It's all good, but more cruelty, PLEASE!

1/19/95 Late night infusion. Sleeping here on the couch, not in the cage, not yet. Too much to do with these drugs and this nervousness I feel. Career is steamrollering ahead—exciting but crushing. *Visiting Hours Revisited* in Boston, February 9. Berlin, February 12. Otis, also in February. Now add Exit Art, to the stew, the performance/ body art retrospective. Interviews. Phone calls. Budgets. And I'm in such a hot mood for sex and submission, but instead I have to work. And what about breathing? Oh, I forgot, I'm sick, yeah. I'm dying, remember? New pieces I want to make. Sue Spaid Gallery. Stuff and stuff and stuff.

1/20/95 Like a camp out here on the couch. Sheree asleep. Me with ear plugs to block that whisper of a snore she has tha unnerves me like so many things unnerve me. Watching *Mir* on tv. Had dinner with Kirby and Rita and watched *Don't Look Back* and *The Wiz Kids* (my term for Maria Beatty and her piss queen mistress). Itchy asshole. Want to be a slave but I'm always uncomfortable, annoyed, distracted, and Sheree's asleep. Me too.

1/21/95 Locked in the cage for two and a half hours bound in strait jacket. Scared at first that I would panic, but it was good. I counted the seconds, I rocked back and forth, and I dwelled on the pain in my lower back and in my right foot against the metal floor. Took deep breaths. Felt calm. Peaceful. Rigged up the video camera so someone could monitor me—baby-sit me—upstairs while Sheree went out, leaving me only slightly unattended. Thought Kirby was going to be the baby-sitter—then I realized Sheree didn't go out like she said she was going to. Kirby was here for a while, too, video taping. Now it's late. I'm tired. Turned on. Doing antibiotics. Scribbling.

1/23/95 Fell asleep on the couch and I forgot to write last night and almost forgot tonight. Wiped out yesterday after the rigors of breathing while trying to supervise Andy cleaning the garage and setting up my office, and Ed accompanying me to the storage space to take inventory for the Boston show. The *Sick Superman* print rattled when I picked it up: broken glass. Panic. Out of breath. But it's OK. But how am I? Bad pain in my chest all day. Felt like collapsed lung or pleurisy. Called Dr. Riker. Supposed to see him tomorrow morning, but after sleeping on the couch awhile I don't feel so bad. Might just be a cracked rib or pulled muscle. I get so fucking worried because I feel so fucking bad. I have so much to do and I feel so lousy—but I don't want to get worse.

1/25/95 Fell asleep on the couch last night and I didn't write. Fell asleep again tonight and I almost forgot, but here I am, nervous wreck all night. Preparing shit for Boston. Truck comes tomorrow. Went to Debbie's tonight, but forgot to refill my oxy-, so I had to drive home huffing and puffing. Everything's a hassle. Shitty shitty mood. But Sheree's completely understanding, no matter how much I rant and rave. She made me dinner. Don't know why I'm so crazy. Can't relax. Can't sleep. Can't stay anywhere. Too much drugs—prescription. Took a Halcyon and I'm going to sleep, even though Halcyon sleep is weird sleep—not restful—but it's the only kind I can get right now.

1/27/95 Dozed on the couch last night doing drugs. Tonight too, but I'm playing through with the scribbling, even at this late hour, and even though I'm zonked. SM panel at Fullerton College tonight with Sheree, Bill S., Ira and his girl toy, Sarah. Bored to tears doing that stuff but this one pays money, so I did it. Ran out of oxygen and Sheree had to run to the car for the spare tank. My lousy breathing is always the main concern. Life is very hard and sometimes it completely panics me.

1/28/95 Took a Halcyon because last night I didn't take a Halcyon and last night I didn't sleep. Aches and pains and complaints. Pain in my right chest, bad all day and night, but now, not so bad. What gives? Depressed as hell. I don't know who I am anymore. I get these nostalgic flashes on the person I used to be—not years ago, *weeks* ago! But I've got my orgasms back. That's something—used to be everything.

1/29/95 By the light of the bedroom tv. Pain in my shoulder. SOB (short of breath) from the long, grueling trip downstairs. Seeing Riker on Tuesday. Sometimes I feel so bad I worry I might go back in the hospital. So today I went to Otis College with Sheree and Ed and set up the casket for next Saturday's show, just in case I'm indisposed during the week. Still have more to do, so I'm not indisposed. Don't think I'll be in the hospital. Nothing they can do. I just feel like shit. Shitty lungs filled with shit and I feel like shit. Anything else to talk about? No.

1/30/95 What do I have to do tomorrow that makes me so nervous tonight? Too much: Doctor's appointment; draft oxygen let ter for Dr. Riker; measure rods for alphabet wall; get gang box for video casket; what thickness are those rods? Fax Pollas; call Exit Art; call Peter; Fedex package to Exit Art—photographs; draft letter of instructions for Boston people; what else needs to be shipped to Boston? Tell Boston about Norm's date for *Why* text; find video for NGBK; ship NGBK video; finish coffin at Otis; find AIG forms for Riker; pick up Rx at Long Beach; double check *Visible Man*; tell Boston about *Visible Man* goop; find coffin video tapes; write checks and mail bills; type up this list. Back to today: Saw Obler. "You have money now," he said when I told him about the cost of Wellbutrin, right after I said we were finally getting some money from our art. Is he feeling taken advantage of by me? Could barely move, I was so short of breath. But I picked up photos on Sunset anyway. Picked up Sheree from work. Had dinner with Jack Skelley. He left. Donna arrived. Troubles in married land, i.e. reality. That does tend to rear its ugly head, doesn't it?

1/31/95 Last day of the first month ends with gloom and doom on the horizon for me. The horrible health (bad breathing and pain) comes off and on, mostly on, and the pulmonary tests at the doctor's echoed what I've been feeling: low and getting lower. I'm dying. It sounds like melodrama, but the damn thing is that it's true—and everyone has to face it: Sheree, my parents, *me*. I'm so sick of the art crap. Sick of *Visiting Hours*. Every day is a pile of work and expectations. Pile of crap. What else do I want to be doing? I don't know—relaxing. Numbness.

February, 1995

2/1/95   Therapist or no therapist, anti-depressant or not, I'm depressed. Angry. Feel like I'm being picked apart by vultures. Everybody wants something and I have nothing to give—or it's such a struggle I just want to shut down. I don't read. I barely brush my teeth. Hate taking showers. Forget shaving. The same clothes every day. The same spot on the couch (when I'm lucky). Crummy, shitty food because I just don't give a damn.

2/2/95   Again by the dim light of the television, dim Bob whines as Sheree snores, but I can't hear the tv cause I don't want to hear Sheree, so I've got earplugs in, which is frustrating because I'd like to hear—bald Dennis Hopper talking to Tom Snyder, but I can't stand the sound of Sheree's snoring—I mean I *really* can't stand it. It unnerves me. I'm the worst snorer in the world, but she doesn't know it cause she's out and I'm up—always up. A nervous wreck. Anti-depressants. Anti-anxiety. Vicodin. Steroids. Feel like crying all the time. Don't want to go on this trip. Gave every last ounce of energy to *Visiting Hours* in New York.—cant give any more. But I'm doing it. I'm hating it and I'm doing it. I took the earplugs out—one earplug so I could hear the tv with one ear, but all I can hear is Sheree—I love her; I want to be with her, but that sound! Argh! I want to scream.

2/3/95   Back in bed. Depression is on full force. Everywhere I look I see shit. Success. Afraid of everything. Mad at everyone. Why hasn't my mother called me lately? Is she mad at me because she thinks I'm mad at her because if I'm depressed that's all she can think is that it's her, it must be her; but it's not her, and it's not Sheree; I don't even think it's me. Sheree says it's cause I'm dying, but I don't even know if that's it. Is it chemical? Drugs? Not enough drugs? Too much (prescription)? Too much tv? Too much thinking? Not enough thought. Where's my wit? Where's my sense of humor? That's a laugh.

2/4/95 Opening night for the Otis show. Lots of people. Many said they liked the coffin. Sheree called Peter Norton "Tom." Dr. Obler came. Said I looked better. Told him how awful it's been. Said to try increasing the Welbutrin. Was horribly anxious today. Letter from Social Security wanting me to come into their office with pay stubs from 93, 94, 95. Yikes. That's scary. So I'm home now. Ran out of oxygen at the opening, came home early—not too early. Sheree came home for a while and now she's at the party and I'm home in my underwear blissfully alone—well, not blissfully, but home, last two days home—before our trip, yikes again.

2/5/95 For someone who's a nervous wreck over having so much to do I've got the balls to spend the day doing practically nothing: computer games, breakfast with Laura Brun and Sheree, anti-anxiety pills, sleep, and tv tv tv. I did do some repair work—not much—on the coffin at Otis. What worries me now? Sheree says Kirby's upset cause he's not included in the Boston opening or its honoraria. He's an equal partner in *Autopsy* isn't he? The world is just too much damn trouble.

2/7/95 Boston. Giant two room suite at Boston Park Plaza, just the two of us. Embarrassment of riches. First class air, but it was-n't all that special, but lots of food and great attention. The exhibit looks good. Small version of *Visiting Hours*. I'm feeling OK, but exhausted. Chest pains. But not anxious. Pills pills pills. Last night, as we were packing to leave, I go to the garage to get y leather jacket, where it's been hanging on an IV pole for weeks, and—surprise surprise—it's gone! Someone walked into our complex, into our open garage, and took my leather jacket. Someone we know? What the fucking hell. Now I'm wearing an old black overcoat like some fucking pervert. Why not?

2/8/95-2/11/95   Berlin. Midnight in Berlin. Sheree's out (of course) investigating an SM club with Ulmann, our contact from the gallery. I'm by myself (what else) here in our hotel room. Not the lavish accommodations we had in Boston, but modern and nice just the same. But I truly hate being here. I just want to be home. Extremely tired. Don't know what time my body's on. Haven't written for the past few days out of complete exhaustion putting up *Visiting Hours* in Boston. Every minute seemed to be filled with working, talking or eating. I don't think my health is too bad for all the wear and tear, I just don't want to be here. Berlin is ugly and depressing. Old American movies on tv. Old—everything seems old, and I don't care about the historical importance or the architecture or the art—it's just old. It all seems so dark and foreboding to me. I wish it were Tuesday already and we were on our way home. Nice attitude, but what can I do? Kevanne is in town. Nice to see her, but rehashing the old days and filling her in on the past three years—good and bad—that's depressing too. Sheree falling asleep while I stay awake—depressing. Even this big old fat cathedral outside our window—that's *really* depressing. Tomorrow's the performance—old work in the old world, but new audience.

2/12/95   Performance done. Not a magical moment, but adequate. Well attended. Most people seemed to like it, at least they said they did. I wish I was better, newer; but all it is is over, and that's good. For the record: Showed *Pigs is Pigs*. With its German little piggies, tiny peasant huts and house frau mamma pit, it was interesting to show this to a German audience. From then on I read the usual bullshit poems—or whatever—trying to get a grasp on the audience. Some laughter. Almost some applause. Appreciative. Did the naked *Body* with live video thing. Sheree on camera, Kevanne with the light. Transformation into "Supermasochist." And then the song *Supermasochistic Bob*... Dinner and talk afterward, just like any reading. Nan Goldin, one of our fans—taking a few pictures. Schnitzel. Nauseous. Tired. Chest and back pain. Back at the hotel, tired but unable or unwilling to sleep—desperate for decent tv. What a genius.

2/13/95 Blah blah blah blah blah blah blah... I'm so sick of talking abut myself. But we give them what they pay for. Interview with woman from Amsterdam. I then did a slide show and talk attended by only five or six people—see, even *they're* sick of us. But we are competing with the Berlin Film Festival. And they did only announce our talk at the last minute. So it was a small but attentive and chatty group. Afterward straight back to the hotel for food and sleep—but neither of us are sleeping. Only hours away from the time to leave—depart—go home. Sheree's dreading the thought of going home. To me it's heaven.

2/14/95 Home is where the heart is on this Valentine's Day. Tv, Sheree snoring, me awake—life goes on. Talked to my mother on the phone. Hard to talk to her for some reason. She seems so fucking distant. What the hell did I do? She's probably thinking the same thing about me.

2/15/95 Strangely depressed. Hate my work. No ideas. All old stuff I've been riding on for two years. My Berlin performance was pathetic, now that I think about it. I'm embarrassed by everything I do.

2/16/95 A bug on me in bed. Itchy all night. Thought it was ants, but this was another kind of a bug, small, round. Are there more? Am I infested with something? I'm thinking about this, sitting up, next to Sheree, her nose in a book, as usual. She says, "Hug me, hug me." And I blow up. Say, "Why? How?" Then I start ranting how she doesn't pay attention to me—but she does—when she's not working or sleeping. I'm such a sullen bastard. God, I can't stand her snoring.

Obviously my ranting didn't phase her. Everything phases me. Soon I'll be phased out.

2/17/95 I don't know when the last time was we had sex. I said that because I'm watching two people fuck on tv. We're close, yeah—closer than ever, in some ways—but physically we don't even know where to start. Anti-depressants? Maybe. Good excuse. But I can't shake my depression. Sheree's great, but I'm wallowing in darkness—true role reversal. Stopped taking Paxil because I couldn't come. Now I can come, but I don't care. Lately I'm not even getting hard. I come, but I don't get hard. No help from Sheree. She's dead asleep. And when she does want to help I run. Last night I snapped her head off because she wanted me to hold her. What kind of jerk am I becoming? Mr. Artist. We get news today of Art Matters grants. $2000 for me, and $1500 each for Sheree and Kirby. But it doesn't lighten my mental load. I'm still full of shit.

2/18/95 Art. $1500 check from Boston. Shit. It was supposed to be $3000. Next time get it in writing. Tom Knetchel at Rosamund Felsen. Pleasant. The best thing is Rosamund asked for my number because she wanted to call me about something. Hmmm... But more openings: Jeanne What's-her-name at Richard Telles. Tense there. All these people we haven't seen in a while. Feeling out of touch, out of the circle. Sheree starting to slip a bit. Find out there's a party afterward which we wouldn't have known about if Sheree hadn't asked. Tense. Home for oxygen, an anxiety pill, and on to the party at Clyde What's-his-name's, very big collector, very upscale party. Everyone we know is there, but we wouldn't have been, would we? Megan's even cold. Is she mad cause I asked her if she saw my jacket anywhere last week? Is she insulted cause she thinks I suspect her? She doesn't think that. I *do* suspect her, but she shouldn't think that. So that adds to the stew of insecurity. But the evening progresses and the drinks are flowing and by the time we leave Sheree's wobbling all over the place drunk. Throws up on the way home. Conks out on the couch but barely rises for Jake, her date for the evening. Out, that's where she is now.

2/19/95   Sex on tv—of course not in real life. All I am is complaints. Even now I'm complaining cause Sheree reads too much and doesn't pay attention to the tv—or me, that's what really matters. Feeling completely crazy today. Anxiety over Ed being here doing his laundry. Anxiety over Gary Indiana and Rita and Kirby and Lloyd. Anxiety over the plumbing going nuts and showering water through the floor, onto the room downstairs for over an hour—that would make anyone crazy, but through it all I just can't breathe and my chest is filled with a sense of doom. Sheree gave me a Librium and I conked out, skipping Rita and Kirby in favor of sleeping on the couch. Wake up to come to bed, watch more tv, and write this, as Sheree sort of touches my back, then keeps quitting, and is probably falling asleep, and that pisses me off, but what doesn't these days?

2/20/95   Bed. Tv. Snoring. Coughing. Felt crazy again today. Saw Obler. Going to try it without anti-depressants. Not doing any good anyway. It's not my head, it's my damn lungs. Nervous all the time because it's so hard to breathe, so hard to move, so hard to talk to people. Don't want to see anyone. Feel lonely, but just want to be left alone. Had dinner with Mike and Anita. That was nice. Always is. They're practical and non-pretentious. Art and life, what a bunch of crap. We're all just Willie Lomax—not art stars. Traveling salesmen getting screwed up the butt. No good writing here. Maybe if I shut the tv off once in a while… no way!

2/22/95   Nothing day. Sleeping most of the time. Stupid OJ trial. Trying to get Shiffler stuff sent out but moving like I'm in Jello. No writing. No reading. No thinking. Dead already.

2/24/95   Lots of tv. Fucking OJ trial. Bad headaches and stomach aches. Went out for a brief lunch with Donna and Sheree on her lunch hour. Could barely eat my soup. Complained and ragged on everything. Came home and threw up. Vicodin and anti-anxiety pills. Don't want the real world. Can't get comfortable. Sheree fights off depression over me, her bum son, Matthew, her oppressive day job. I can be depressed but *not* her. She gives me a massage tonight but I complain all the way through it. I *do* feel better though. Now she's asleep and I wish she wasn't. She said she'd rather whip me than massage me. This morning I masturbated fantasizing about her whipping me but now, in reality, I push it off. Why? Why don't I give into it anymore? Afraid. Terrified. Chicken shit. So I'm here in bed alone while she sleeps on the couch, both of us disappointed as hell, on that long road of depression. Gotta change it somehow. Gotta feel better. Somehow. But how? More tv.

2/25/95 Saturday night dead. The day drags on and on until it ends as it started—in bed, in front of the tv. Slept on the couch a little. Worked on the computer a little. Breakfast with Sheree. The nagging depression, or whatever it is.
Emotional numbness. Alone. But don't want to be with anyone, not now. Sheree's out. A conference for trans-gender types—where everyone and her mother wants to be a guy, when they all hate guys to begin with. I stay home, screen calls and watch a movie about a Russian serial child killer. Fun stuff.

2/27/95 Ants eat my phlegm. Why? Cause I'm so good. Actually, I don't feel so bad tonight—mood wise. Been sort of goofy. Playing "Myst" on the computer. Saw Dr. Obler. Talked about Mom, who's pissing me off. Talked about money, credit cards. Sometimes he seems so judgmental it makes me feel nervous and stupid. Guilty. I never thought much of people who feel guilty, but here I am feeling guilty all the time. Guilty about pulling a fast one on the credit card companies by dying before I pay them. Maybe I'm just guilty about dying—period. Leaving everybody, and being a shit in the process, complaining all the time, writing

this poop, and doing nothing but watching this crap tv—
Letterman, OJ, dead air—anything and nothing.

2/28/95   Headaches, chest aches, side aches, ass aches—aside
from that, I'm feeling better. Short of breath—what else? Did
some business with the cars today. Talked to Deborah Drier today.
Talked to my Mom today—no we're not mad at each other. My
problem is me. I'm mad at what's happening to me—not at her or
Dad or Sheree. She's got to let me express how I feel without taking it personally or making it into something it isn't. It was a good
talk, something that's been coming on for a while. We're all in for
some rough times ahead. Take your Prozac.

3/1/95 New month. Same old Bob. I can't wait to come to bed, get under the covers and watch tv all night. Too bad there isn't something better on. But I'll watch any old shit, doesn't matter—it's the watching that matters. Eyes forward. Mind ass-backwards. Here's a movie with Donald Sutherland— stopped writing cause I was watching—*Benefit of the Doubt*. He's a killer—I just bet. Tomorrow, the OJ Trial. Real life—sort of. Real killers. I predict here, on March 1, that OJ will go crazy before he goes to jail. Sheree's in snoresville. How can I put earplugs in to block out the snoring and still hear the tv? The insignificant problems of significant others.

3/2/95 In bed, late night, in front of the tv, thinking about my life and what a loser I could easily be, what a fluke it is that I'm not. I still don't really have a job or a marketable skill. This art thing is a fluke. So I sold a couple of pieces. I may never sell anything again. So all my expenses are covered—there wouldn't be any expenses if I didn't do art. Nothing I do pays the rest of the bills. I'm still on SSI—and now they have questions about my art income, what they perceive as income. Now I'm in big trouble with them. If it weren't for Sheree I'd be living in a shit hole with nothing—not even the art. And basically, if I were to live longer than two more years, I'd have to do something else financially because my share of it still sucks. These are the pleasant thoughts that occupy my mind late at night, in between flashes of old sitcoms. Ha ha ha.

3/4/95 Rainy weekend. S asleep upstairs. B barely awake here. She was gone all day at art school helping to choose next year's suckers. Today I had breakfast with Donna, and a movie— *Exotic*—but Donna was late and the movie was sold out, so no movie. Tea instead. That Donna. Pissed me off today. Now I'm dozing. Tv of course.

3/5/95 Sunday stupid Sunday. Tired again, as usual. Debbie's in the morning. Brought bagels home. Actually did something. Went to MOCA with Sheree, Kirby, Kirby's kids, over my protestations cause it was raining, my chest was hurting, didn't want to go out, didn't want to see anybody—just wanted to stay home with Sheree. So I'm yelling and yelling. But I go. Video installations—technically brilliant but mostly unimaginative— but then perhaps I'm *too* imaginative.

3/6/95 Monday: Obler day. Talked about what a bad person I think I am these days. How my body is driving me crazy. How I hate the way I treat Sheree at the same time I'm extremely pro- tective of her and hate the thought of any one not treating her right or misunderstanding her or judging her—and what the fuck do I do? Turn around and do all of these things and hate myself for it. Hate myself for so many things. So many things not done. Running out of time and energy. Saw Kirby's film, recent cut. It's shaping up. Sheree makes it. Her insight is what drives it. Me—I'm just me. It'd be pointless without her insight, with- out her direction—literally. No matter how much I complain about it at the time—she's the one who drives me and I'd be nowhere without her.

3/7/95 Didn't call Bob Crabb. Didn't call Sarah. Didn't contact Ulmann. Didn't contact Lisa in Boston, nor did I send her the invoice I forgot to send last week. Out of touch with Laura. Should call Carol Carompass about Thursday. Haven't returned Scott's call. Gotta mail that stupid check to that stupid woman in New York, and mail my car registration too. When was the last time I called Mom? Never did get back to Dennis. Forgot about Tosh. Almost didn't pick up the phone when Paige called until I found out she was calling from Japan. Supposed to talk to Tosh about going to Japan—urgh! We did, however, have Dinner with Donna and Jessica, someone who works with Jeffrey. A fan from the Moguls performance. On her way to being a Hollywood literary agent. Sheree starts the sit-com rap. Hates her job and I'm supposed to magically get her out of it with some non-existent writing ability that nobody in the sit-com industry would give a shit about, and that's just fine with me because I'm not wasting what little time I have left kissing their asses in this fucking shit business—and fuck—what do I have to do to prove myself already? Yeah, I guess Sheree *is* difficult to be with sometimes.

3/8/95 Lisa calls from the Boston show to ask some questions about taking it down. She tells me someone was there asking about me: Andy Cochran, from high school. So I called him tonight. He's totally unchanged. Lonely. Nerdy. Hasn't heard from Becky. I might be able to contact Kathy Ryan. Terrible headaches. In and out of irritability. Stomach aches. Sheree's snoring. Kirby's schedule. Punching bag design. The Simpson trial. Jerk anesthesiologist from Miami glomming onto me. His stupid fax. His stupid ideas. She's snoring.

3/9/95 My arms are dangerously skinny—scary looking. Can wrap my fingers around my upper arm. That often coincides with a trip to the hospital—damn that snoring—between headaches, chest aches, shortness of breath, stomach aches, loss of weight, depressing irritability and exhaustion, the hospital's probably not too far off. I did manage to do an art talk with Sheree at Otis. And then I met with a few students individually and talked about their work. Sort of like being on a blind date—blind dates, four in a row. "What do I say now?" "Do I sound like a jerk?" I was worried about it but I guess it worked out OK. Bed now. Letterman. Dandruff on my pillow. Bad handwriting. Sheree's snoring. Tired eyes.

3/10/95 My irritability and depression is amok. I feel like crying all the time. I can barely control my penis. My computer keeps crashing, which is exactly how I feel. I hate when people call me on the phone, yet I feel so alone. So distant from Sheree, but she annoys the hell out of me, but I miss her, and love her, and feel sorry for her that she has to be around me. I'm beginning to hate myself. I've *been* hating myself, and it's been lasting a long time now, at least as long as I've been writing this journal—since Christmas, since I've been off anti-depressants. Time to go back? I guess. Will it help? Is all this O^2 related? Not enough? Too much? No answers. Tv is on but I can't hear it because I've got earplugs in my ears to block out Sheree's snoring. I want to run upstairs and fiddle with the computer to get it working again so at least something's back on track, but it's too late (4 am). I *was* asleep but I woke up an hour ago with an awful stomach ache and the usual heartache. Don't know what to do with myself. Took a couple of anti- anxiety pills, but they only make me sleepy *and* anxious. I guess I'm really into the pills now. The age old quest for happy pills. Ain't none. My body throbs with unhappiness. It's not directed at anyone in particular—it really boils down to how I feel physically. It's like a big weight, a giant distraction all the time. So I'm always annoyed by it, antago- nized from the minute I wake up, till the time I finally go to sleep—doesn't leave room for much of anything else.

3/11/95 Always seems like I've got a million things to do, pills to take, treatments, Debbie, people who want to talk to me, eating, sleeping, Sheree, people who want me, anxious and out of breath just thinking about living. Life itself is getting awful. My com- puter keeps crashing. Been up since the last entry going crazy with it. A mirror of my own state of mind.

3/12/95 That's it. Tonight, sleeping pills. Maybe it's the trouble- some computer, or my troublesome in and out hack hack breath- ing—or maybe I'm just nuts, but I haven't been able to sleep. Got the computer back in form, now how about me? Called

Crabb tonight, finally. See Obler tomorrow. Bed bed bed. Sleep—I hope.

3/13/95 Started Zoloft today, antidepressant. Feeling so fucking crazy. Nervous and irritable. And then I can't sleep. Feeling a little calmer now, and Sheree's snoring may send me soaring— again—how to watch tv *and* wear these anti-Sheree plugs in my ears.

3/15/95 More of same bullshit feelings. Throbbing eyes. Headache. Deep—pressure. Deep. Won't go away. Something not connected write in my head. Not enough O too? 2 much? Where's everybody I know? No. So much core respond dance neglected. Work to doo doo. Too much trial watching. Juice. Stuck in the computer, too. Keeps crashing—like me. Trying to finish these punching bag ideas, even though there's no Sue Spaid no more. So stupid. Like this writing. Not a writer anymore. What else can I do? Physically unable to anything—comfortably. Have to pull it together—snoring Sheree snoring Sheree. My head to the page. Paging Sheree. Breathing worse than mine. I'm just more sensitive, more awake, more of a shit.

3/17/95 St. Patrick's Day drinks at Kirby and Rita's. Argumentative and picky, whiny me. Irritated all the time. Ed comes over and *really* bugs me. 3 am tv now. Really where I want to be.

3/18/95 Wide—well, not wide—awake at 3:30 am. No matter how deep asleep, or for how long, I always wake up at 3 or 3:30, and don't go back to sleep for an hour or so. No wonder I'm an irritable fuck. Soft core and sexy 976 ads on all night tv—who cares? Bob and Dixie came up to see the casket piece and have dinner. I don't think they get what I do, but OK. Fighting vicious stomach aches and nausea all day and night. The Zoloft? Pain in my left side. Kidneys? Ulcer? Who knows? Who cares?

3/19/95   Up again at 3 am—what gives? Sound asleep since 11. Up at 3, no matter what. Thought I'd escape writing tonight, but found myself mulling over why it is I don't like pain anymore. I have this performance to do on April 1st, and I'm shying away from doing or having SM stuff done to me because pain and the thought of pain mostly just irritates and annoys me rather than turns me on. But I miss my masochistic self. I hate this person I've become. And what about my reputation? Everything I say to people is all a lie, or at least two years too late—what the... ? Not 3 am. Only 1:30 am. Can't even tell time. I knew it was earlier cause the tv was all wrong.

3/21/95   Sheree would note that today is Matthew's birthday. But for me it's only Tuesday, another unproductive day. Went to the doctor's. Will have to check into the hospital at some point, but not quite yet. Scott came over tonight. Had dinner at Red Lion and watched *Natural Born Killers* on laser. Good for the first 45 minutes. Dull after that. Sheree's stoned nagging about the Otis show. Why does she have to take everything I do so personally? Why does she have to possess it all and not leave any room for me or the process. She stifles me so I don't want to commit to any of it. I don't know how I'm going to feel or what I want to do and I don't owe anything to anybody. If I don't perform—so what? Tonight she says, if she's not in my performance, then maybe I shouldn't be in her house. Let *that* be duly noted.

3/22/95   The computer's fixed and Sheree's still on her high horse, higher than ever. Finally faxed Kevanne in Prague, Barbara in Geneva. Lots of calls I didn't pick up on the machine. Pissed at Sheree cause she's still pissed at me over the Otis performance and what I may or may not do. It makes no sense. Why have herself so personally wrapped up in an idea that was mine from the start and is still mine to do or not do depending on what I think I'm able to handle? As of this moment *everything* is a chore. And I no longer feel I owe anything to any audience. No, the show must *not* go on at any cost—in the end, nobody gives a fuck anyway—except Sheree, and she's pissed cause that's not enough. But the truth is, no matter what I do, if I do it for Sheree, it's never enough. There's always some other plateau I didn't strive for, or some rock I didn't crawl under. Our happiness shouldn't be so dependent on our public personalities. Fuck the public. Where's the pubic?

3/24/95 In bed reading computer books, falling asleep. Slept last night on the couch. Bad stomach aches all day, every day. Poked around on the computer all day. Tried to make a flip book of my penis getting nailed. Cold wind outside. Wondered several times during the day where my masochism went, my love for sensation. Soon Sheree will begin her night of lumber jack slumber, sawing wood. Ear plug time. Stomach—ow!

3/25/95 Almost depressing Saturday. Lonely, but I don't want to go anywhere. Skip Arnold had an opening, but I hate openings, and I'm not crazy about Skip's work. So I stayed home. Stomach ache—still. Slept on the couch awhile. Worked (work?) on the computer, trying to learn Illustrator. Thai food with Sheree, then the two of us went over to Rita and Kirby's to watch *Exotic*. OK, but not great. Falling asleep. Sheree's upstairs on the couch. Tv off, but soon to be on. Reading *Illustrator* book, but not for long.

3/26/95 Leave Sheree and Jake upstairs watching gay SM video's while I retire to bed and the *Illustrator Bible*. SM video's are always kind of boring and frustrating. I'm getting a better feeling about Saturday's voyeur show. I'm just going to do the things I used to do to jack off. Ball stretching, butt plugs, enemas, bondage, whipping, nailing—my usual bag of tricks.

3/27/95 How convenient, on a night when I'm too tired to write and shine it on, to wake up suddenly at 2 am—I guess cause I couldn't breathe, cause there was my nasal canula on the floor. So after a tough pee and some ruminations about Saturday's upcoming hotel performance, I thought I might as well write, the only writing I seem to be able to do. Will I ever do real writing again? I'm stuck in this computer graphics mode. I just keep thinking I don't want to stop for anything else, mail I have to mail, calls I have to make, life. Looks like we won our *Saturday Night Live* suit. $3,500-$4000. More computer equipment! Went to an Oscar watching party with Kirby tonight. Money people for one of his film projects. Awful people. Awful show despite Dave Letterman. Boring. TV is boring, but I can't stop watching it. It's on now, even though I can't hear it with these earplugs. Time to flip channels.

3/28/95 Headache. And the fucking computer's not working right... Working on the punching bag image, but now I can't. Driving Ed to the airport tomorrow. He's going to Japan. Sheree's being mean about it, and I'd rather not leave the house, but people are always helping me—it's payback time. But for now, I've been awake since 2 AM—gotta sleep.

3/31/95 Good, last day of March. The days just race by, but each one's like the rest, nothing done, complain, complain, complain. Did I die? Haven't written here the past couple of days cause I've been falling asleep instead. Barely awake now. Me and my exhausting schedule. Depressed again. Losing weight. Tomorrow the Otis performance. Don't think Sheree loves me anymore. She's distant. Not so helpful to me as she was. Seems resentful of something. Depressed herself. But I need her, damn it. Feel abandoned.

April, 1995

4/1/95 Hotel performance done. People watching me from one hotel room while I performed supposedly auto-erotic activities in my own room, all alone. Don't know who saw what, or what anyone thought, or what it all meant. I'm just glad it's over. Wine enema, butt plug, alligator clips, ball whacking, piss drinking, masturbating, bondage—they wanted a show, I gave them a show. Felt disoriented and depressed through most of it, as I feel disoriented and depressed through most everything these days. No more commitments! Sheree doesn't seem to give a shit about me anymore. I'm mad at her about it.

4/2/95 You—whoever you are—must be sick to death of me in front of the TV in bed, every night, describing Sheree's snoring and whining about how awful I feel. Sometimes I don't feel so bad—but then I have to do something, like go from point A to point B. Didn't get to sleep till 3 AM last night—4 AM daylight savings. Here I am tonight, 12:30. Her snoring. Still plugging away at the punching bag design. Don't know what I'm doing. Hearing more good reports about last night's show. Was feeling kind of depressed about it. Thought maybe it was stupid—maybe it still is, but no one's telling me. Ear plugs.

4/3/95 Bills paid. Saw Obler. Doubled my Zoloft. Our work returned from Boston. Hope it's all there. Storage space full. Depression lifting—maybe—a little.

4/4/95 About ready to check into the hospital. Maybe Thursday or Friday. Not breathing well. Pain in left chest. Weight loss. Tired. Time to go. I'm more and more afraid each time that this time I'll get admitted and won't come out. So I hold back, try to finish up what I can around here. Worked on the computer today. Confetti casket. Scanned in a bunch of photos. Watched TV with Sheree. Women who suddenly remember in therapy that they were sexually abused as children. Another show about John Lee Hooker. I didn't want to watch it cause I thought I didn't like his music, but I was wrong—I was thinking of Dr. John—it's Dr. John I don't like. But John Lee Hooker was good, at least in his early days. Weren't we all good in our early days?

4/5/95 Hardly slept at all last night and I'm up late again. Most likely going into the hospital tomorrow morning. Just can't hack it. So short of breath sometimes it gets really scary. Heart pounding. Headache. Buying a new Powerbook computer tomorrow. Maybe I'll get some writing done. But now I'll stop.

4/6/95 The hospital—finally. Seems like I've been talking about coming here ever since the last time I left here. Haven't been breathing or feeling well the whole time and will probably never breathe well or feel well again. I'm not being pessimistic when I say it's only going to get worse. That's the reality. My blood gasses are much worse: PO2 81, PCO2 57. Don't know if that's forever, but it's fucked. Really tired. Done for the day.

4/7/95 Hospital. Wake up at 3:30 in time to make a note here about something, anything. Headache. How about something else, something good. Sheree picked up and brought me the new Powerbook today. Feel guilty and uncomfortable about the expense, but ideally I can use it to write when I'm here—but so far all I've done is play games.

so what does it mean to be here in the hospital again, not breathing?
SWEAT HEAD

keep sweating nit wit nothing to write oj oj oj all day coughing and not writing now not now such a drag when does it happen when does it begin

So now that I have this computer here what do I do with it besides play computer games? Where did all that writing come from. Why won't my fingers or my mind work. I can't even type.

4/8/95 I have to write about being collected. Sort of like being a slave. Art slave. Sheree's slave, her pet. We have a cage and all that. I threw up in it on St. Patrick's day, last year. This year I was not feeling well enough to do anything on St. Patrick's day, or any day. But I still want to be in the cage for an extended period of time. 3 days feels right. After 3 weeks in the hospital, what's 3 days in a cage? What's that movie/book, *The Collector*? There wasn't a cage in that movie, though. I'm thinking of *Lady in a Cage*. And it wasn't a cage, it was an old elevator.

4/9/95 I'm in the hospital. So what else is new? Illuminated by my computer screen. I've been bringing computers to the hospital with me for more than ten years. I'm back here for the sixth or seventh time in a year. I'm averaging every two months. I was in here last Valentine's Day, as well as Thanksgiving. Next week will be Easter, and I'll probably still be here.

4/10/95 Still hospitalized. Didn't feel like writing the past two days. Not much happening. Feeling somewhat better. Headaches still. "Pain Management" doctor concerned about all the Vicodin. Knows nothing about CF. Asshole. I just got done yelling at a respiratory therapist for leaving me here with no O^2 for 15 minutes while he was out of the room doing whatever. This same guy has done the same thing to me several times before. How would they like to sit here for 15 minutes with a plastic bag over their heads? Feel guilty for blowing up, but they can't keep doing that. Ah, what the hell, I feel good blowing up. Sheree and Kirby were here today. Yesterday, Phil and L.R.—Bill Sine and his "Bob Fest" idea. Please don't make me the center of attention just because I'm sick. It's ok if I do it, but not from the outside in. What?

4/11/95 So what not much. In the hospital. The sun's too bright. We don't need a cloud. Investigate. Testimony. Illness.

4/12/95 So the doctor says I'll be around awhile. Not dying yet, even though I might feel like it. Even though I might wish for it. Even though I've got all these credit card bills filled to the max.

I'm taking a new pill that's supposed to help me sleep, so of course here I am, 3:30 AM, writing and sweating and thinking and peeing. I use the urinal at night cause I'm too lazy to go to the bathroom. Nothing wrong with me. Going home Friday. Even Dr. Riker says he thinks I'll be around till next year at least. But they want me to cut down on the Vicodin. Afraid I'm getting addicted.

4/13/95 Before I die. just let me say one thing. What do I do now? "It makes for a very unproductive day." Well that's the way they wanted it. They lied over and over and over. A brand new box of rubber gloves. Protection for everybody. Phlegm. Bob Phlegmagain.

Last night here (hospitalized.) 2 AM. Drenched in sweat. Had to change my gown and have the nurse change the sheets cause they were soaked. Something to do with the pills they're giving me. Zipamine, or somethng, an anti-depressant, but low dose. It's supposed to bring back endorphins that have supposedly been knocked off by all the Vicodin I've been taking. That couldn't be bad. Wouldn't hurt to get some endorphins back. But meanwhile, a side effect is I'm drenched in sweat. Talked to Deborah Drier today. She met Ira Silverberg, and Amy Gerstler was there, and somehow my name came up and Amy gave her my number here. Sheree's picking me up tomorrow. She says she misses me, but she sounds depressed. Karmen's spending the weekend. What set off Sheree's depression, I wonder? She says she doesn't know, but I'm sure I'll find out.

4/14/95 Home from the hospital. 2 AM. Crazy drug schedule. Sheree upstairs with Karmen, house guest for the weekend. Watched video's at Mike Kelley's with him, Anita, Jim and Marnie, Rita and Kirby, Jake and Karmen. Eyes tired. Home.

4/15/95 Late again (2:30.) SM party for crazy Sharon. I didn't want to go because I never want to go anywhere. But it was ok. Nice people. I don't care much for watching people play SM at parties. I either feel bored, left out, or intrusive. Sheree zoning out again. She seems to interpret "stress leave" as time to not go to work so she can stay home and dwell on things to be stressed and depressed about. So after a week of her moaning about my being away from her—I'm home—and she's as distant as hell. Shit. I would rather have stayed in the hospital. I don't need the stress.

4/16/95 End of Easter. Late again. Drugs. Saw *Portishead* with Scott, Sheree and Karmen. Sheree's upstairs with Karmen. Sounds like she's whipping her. Just got done cutting her. Wanted to cut me, but I said no. Over and over again cause she's stoned and won't take no for an answer. I feel guilty and unfulfilled saying no. But I'm tired. That's a good excuse. I'm stupid—that's a better one.

4/17/95 I don't get many visitors when I'm in the hospital, and most of the time that's fine with me. It's an awkward situation all around and on both sides of the bed nobody feels good.

More late night drugs. No going out tonight—good. Sexy women, scantily clad, some horror movie on TV. Sheree's snoresville. Karmen back home. Besides doing drugs most of the day I've been playing/ working on the computer—the punching bag design, blackjack, and a little writing. Writing about the hospital. I seem to have more energy than I've had in a while. Just need to focus somehow.

4/20/95 Haven't written in the journal for the past three nights because I haven't been downstairs for three days because I keep falling asleep on the couch while running my antibiotics. Since I don't finish up until 2 am and have start all over again four hours later, there's not much sense in going down stairs. But I might tonight. Drove Sheree down to Irvine, to school, even though that was the last thing I wanted to do, but she was sick all day and wasn't going to go, and then she got stoned and started feeling guilty about not going but too stoned to drive, so I drove her, after much bitching and whining cause she was driving me crazy in her stoned state, but I drove her, and waited for her, still residual slave stuff inside there somewhere.

4/21/95 Four nights and I still haven't been downstairs — wait — last night after writing here, and after running the three antibiotics, I did go downstairs to bed, forgot. After all these years, I still miss it when I don't sleep with Sheree, even with her snoring. But right now I'm still up here, upstairs, computer on the coffee table, and the pile of usual shit, and the constant tv, bombing news, tragedy, nuts, psychopaths, can't tear myself away. And of course, OJ. Went to dinner with Sheee, Molly, Murray, Richard and Ted. Met Donna and Jeff at the Nuart afterwards to see Michael Powell's *Stairway to Heaven*. Dated but brilliant, like me. Let the drugs flow. I have to go.

4/22/95 Another night of drugs on the couch after a Saturday of laziness. I finally took a shower, but that was about it. Just drugs. But tonight Sheree's sleeping on the couch — and snoring! Ahhhh. She won't go to bed. Ahhhhh.

4/23/95 Here again. Drugs. Computer. TV. Couch. Naked. Alligator clip on my dick. Fantasize about putting dozens and dozens of clips on my dick, but I can barely stand one. Trying to get this writing thing going. My fingers don't work on these keys. Maybe I'm just a lousy typist? Maybe I'm just a lousy writer. How would I know when I hardly ever write? Headaches headaches headaches. Sheree in bed. She handcuffed me today while she went out with Rita. We both liked that. Can we get our mistress/slave thing back? How can it work with me barely able to stand anything or do anything?

4/24/95 Here I am tippydetyping on the couch cause I'm still on the drugs, nothing interesting, just antibiotics. Lately I've been longing for Demerol. Reminiscing about those days of post surgery when I got it when I wanted it and I liked it — a little too much. But, ho hum, nothing but Tobramycin, Piperacillin and Ceftazidime in my veins. A couple of Vicodin in my mouth, but that doesn't do much anymore beyond dulling the headache, which is fine I suppose. Sheree's here on the couch too. Not sleeping cause she slept till noon today. She's out on stress leave so she has no schedule. She's waving her naked legs in the air. She's reading about gardening, her new hobby. I want her to put dozens of alligator clips on my dick and balls, but I don't know if I'd freak out or not. I can put a couple on myself. It hurts like hell but most of the time I can hold on until the pain subsides and I get kind of a rush. But can I take it when she's in control? The ultimate question.

4/25/95 Letterman. Couch. Drugs. How we do drag on. Getting hard to breathe again. Thought I was doing much better. It never lasts. My mood has been better, though. And I've got a renewed interest in sex, mostly fantasizing about this alligator clip thing, and trying it out a little bit with a couple of clips here and there, those jagged little teeth biting into my tender spots as I grab hold of something like the bed rail and squeeze until the pain floats off a little, turns sweet almost, and then it's time for another. It's almost like eating hot chili peppers, except these taste buds are in my balls.

4/26/95 Itchy eyes. Can't focus. Tired… again. On the couch… again. Drugs… again. And I'm still into this alligator clip thing. Last night, after I finally went down to bed, I put seven of them on my dick — along the shaft, on the corona and the tip of the head — and I kept them there — and I came (well, it's a pathetic form of coming, but I came). Now I'm ready for Sheree to go at me with even more clips for a longer period of time, and then hot wax afterwards. We would have done it tonight but she had to go to school and I had to go to Debbie's, then there's these stupid drugs to do — we're exhausted, as usual. I'll probably dabble with a few of them again tonight, just to stay in shape: alligator clip training.

4/27/95 Last night for antibiotics. This time around. Last call for Demerol (I wish). Don't need pain killers now. I'm a masochist again! Thirteen alligator clips after last nights entry. Wasn't as turned on as I was the previous night, but the discipline is still there. The obsessiveness, which I've missed. Tomorrow Sheree leaves for Oregon for a few days. I have it in my head to do a few things to myself, if I don't chicken out or tire out or crap out. The world is blowing up around me, but I shall be entertained.

4/28/95 No more drugs. But I'm still here on the couch, naked, tv on, coffee table full of junk, headache. Sheree in Oregon. She just called, stoned, talking about art again, mad at me again cause I didn't like whatever idea she was going on about. Trapped. I went for the cheese once again. Rats. All's well otherwise. Still in the mood for torture. I always get it into my head to eat shit when Sheree out of town and I'm here alone left to my own devices. I never have been able to go through with it. I haven't even tried it in years. But I've got some energy now, and I'm in a mood, and it's still a cherry I haven't plucked. But it's so disgusting. Auto-humiliation. The plan is to handcuff myself with my hands behind my back in the cage with a plate full of my own shit in front of me. Embedded throughout the shit is a string of five candy Lifesavers tied together with fishing line and fed through a hole in the plate, down and out of the cage, up and over and back down again suspended over my back. On the end of the line is the handcuff key and the cage key. When I finally get my nerve up and eat through the shit I find the Lifesavers and suck them until they melt, one by one, freeing the fishing line so it pulls through the hole in the plate, allowing the hand-cuff key to drop down behind my back to my waiting hands where I then unlock myself and let myself out of the cage, feeling thoroughly disgusted with myself, but at the same time turned on and strangely filled with an overwhelming sense of accomplishment. But talk is cheap.

4/29/95 Can hardly keep my eyes open. It's not real late, but I'm still tired. No shit eating tonight. Lots to do. Video to set up. Have to take my time and not get too tired. Can't even write I'm so tired.

4/30/95 Let the shit eating begin. I'm downstairs, in bed, watching tv. Tv keeps me grounded and keeps my mood up. Setting up these elaborate auto-erotic sm scenarios is by nature isolating and lonely. Tv, and its window on the "normal" helps keep the depression at bay. Shit is disgusting. It's supposed to be. That's why the need for all the padlocks, keys, handcuffs, fishing line, rope, etc. Once I cross that line and snap those locks, there's no way out but to eat shit. Literally "eat shit or die." No matter how much I fantasize about this ultimate degradation, no matter how much the thought of it gets me hard, I always chicken out at the moment of truth. The couple of times in the past when I've done the hidden keys and padlock thing, I very Houdini-like, managed to escape without a bite, feeling very stupid, very humiliated — as humiliated by what I almost did as I was for not having the guts to do it. But tonight is different. I think I've completely out-smarted myself. I'll be in bondage from head to toe, no way out until I eat through this big pile of my own shit, find the hidden Lifesavers which are tied to fishing line, suck the Lifesavers until they melt, freeing the line and allowing the keys to drop down behind my back, where I can then unlock my handcuffs, ankle restraints and nose pierce. Assuming I don't chicken out. I've been assembling this coropheliac contraption for three days. I can't back out now. That would make me a failure. It's hard enough being such a weirdo, I don't want to be a failed weirdo.

All that for one lousy little bite. I'm only a partial failure. The best laid plans of perverts… First of all the bondage was a little too much. I was afraid that once I tied my nose down and locked my hands behind my back that I wouldn't be able to breathe. Very uncomfortable. But that was the idea, right? But the biggest flaw was the Lifesavers. They dissolved in the shit before I ever got to them. Why the keys didn't drop right away, I don't know. I had to push the shit away with my face and nudge the line with my tongue. And that's another design problem. That's what tying my nose down was supposed to circumvent, but even after I tied it it came loose right away. I didn't have to eat the shit at all. All I had to do was push it aside with my face. Back to the drawing board. But I did get two good bites out of it. Tastes like mud. Bitter mud. Felt stupid at the sight of my shit covered face in the mirror. But I'll try it again. Keep doing it until I get it right.

5/1/95 Needless to say, I didn't get much sleep last night. Lots of running around today. Riker. Obler. Homeowner's meeting. Didn't want to tell Obler about the shit eating. Who can I tell if I can't tell my psychiatrist? I have a hard time talking about sex with him. I did tell him I was into an SM frame of mind again, especially with Sheree being away. He questioned why I felt sexier with Sheree gone. I think it's like being a kid again, with the parents out. I've got the whole place to myself to run wild and do my strange masterbatory things. But I couldn't say I eat shit. And I'm not satisfied with the shit eating I did do. I think I know how to redo it, and I thought about doing it tonight, to rectify this failed experiment in excrement, but I'm exhausted. Maybe tomorrow, during the day. Besides there's no shit to eat, not yet.

5/2/95 In bed with Sheree of all people. Home from Oregon. Crazy night of bells and whistles. All I wanted was a couple of egg rolls. But I burnt them, and then the smoke alarm goes off, and then the oven starts beeping and won't stop and the gas won't shut off. Searching frantically for the owner's manual. When I find it it says to unplug it and call a service person. So I shut down the electricity to the oven and everything calms down, but not me. Hard time breathing today. Slight fever. Too much shit this weekend?

5/3/95 In bed again with the practically comatose Sheree. It bugs me that she can go to sleep so fast at night. When she's out of town at least I know she's gone. But here I think she's here but she's gone. I'm watching tv and she's — I don't know where. Complain complain. I just want more sex. SM shit. If she's here I want it with her. If she's not, I just want it. But all day I felt like too much crap for anything. Feverish. Short of breath. Sweating buckets. Sort of worried that I fucked myself up with this shit stuff, but I'm always sick so who knows what it's from. If I die I die. But right now I'll just watch tv and sleep. Then Sheree will probably wake up.

5/4/95 Mom's birthday. Faxed her a birthday card with my face Photoshopped over the bodies of little cherubs sitting on the words "Happy Birthday." Just what every mother wants. John, the son a bitch, didn't even have the decency or balls to call her. I have to write to that fucker and tell him what I think of him and his fucking religion. Still short of breath today. The oven man came. Someone stole my car battery cause it's parked on the street cause it's leaking oil all over the carports. Tom came over tonight and we watched *Seinfield*, then he drove Sheree to a party at Cathy Opie's. I didn't want to go. I love staying home. Don't even want to talk to anyone. Idea for a new performance and new work, some of which I'm already working on: *Bob Flanagan's Toyland*. I can redesign all kinds of toys to tie me up and torture me in front of a live audience. Good show for Christmas.

5/5/95 Tish's birthday. Lazy day again. Sweating and sleeping. Flying to Mom's tomorrow with Sheree and Kirby. Didn't get anything for her birthday. Sent her a bunch of money last week. That's good. But am I good? I'm dirty. Need a shower or a bath, but in the morning I'm too cold and I want to get upstairs to the couch or the computer. And at night I'm too tired. So I'm dirty. And I never, hardly ever, brush my teeth any more. There's no sense going to the dentist. I just hope the teeth hang on as long as I do. So maybe I should brush them once in a while. Showed Kirby the shit notes and the b/w shit tape. Of course he thought

[48]

it was gross. What else could it be? But I can't wait to do it again. Maybe at Mom's. Naw. But I did have a dream last night that I was shitting on the toilet at her house with the door open and she caught me. I think I was excited by that. A sicko even in my dreams.

5/6/95 Mom and Dad's house in Arizona. Tension thick. Feel like I am caught shitting. This stuff with John not calling shades everything. Elly's family was here too for dinner. Nice people, I guess. Most importantly, good friends to Mom and Dad; but strangers to us, and loud, and obnoxious. I'm sorry, I had nothing to say to them. After a barbeque we all high tail it out of there, Sheree, Tim, Kirby and me. We go to the movies. Thought I wanted to see *While You Were Sleeping*. Yuck! Syrupy unfunny crap with more loud and obnoxious families. Sneak over to Carpenter's remake of *Children of the Damned*. All the time though I'm nervous cause I know Mom's upset that we left, even though she didn't say anything, and even though I asked her if cared if we went to the early or late show. No she didn't, but yes she did. Don't we ever grow up? Into the shit pot with every little one of life's offenses. Tonight Kirby and Sheree interviewed Tim and me for the documentary. Tomorrow it's Mom and Dad's turn. I doubt they'll be completely honest or forthcoming with their feelings, but we'll see.

5/7/95 Home from Mom's. In bed with Sheree. Loud tv. Remote lost. Tired. Lots of emotion this weekend. Some of it captured on tape by Kirby. Tim still has so much anger about the past. He's still fighting for all the injustices he feels were done to him as a child. Even though we all admit we made mistakes and were all doing the best we could do with what we knew how to do at the time, Tim is still fucked up over the past. Sometimes there's such a look of hatred in his eyes when he looks at me I want to get the hell out of there. So I try to make light of the situation. Tell jokes. Change the mood of the room. But that only makes it worse. Ah well. Tomorrow we all retreat to our mutual shrinks.

5/8/95 Mom calls in tears over the weekend and Tim. I feel horrible about it. What kind of an idiot is Tim anyway that he can't
look around him and see what's going on. He's not a fucking kid
anymore. I want to tell him what I feel, but it will only lead to a
huge fight and he withdrawing completely and Mom's already
got that from John, she doesn't need it from Tim too. But she
doesn't need this either. Talk about fucked up families and sib-
ling shit: just saw *Crumb* with Kirby and Rita. Not the great documentary everyone said, but it was good. Sad. Ours will be much
better.

5/9/95 Typing while Sheree snaps pictures of me naked in bed.
We got new haircuts today. She keeps saying I look cute. That's
it. That's all I did today was get a haircut—and go to Debbie's.
Gotta get more productive. But I've been having trouble breathing again. All I like to do is lie on the couch and watch the OJ
trial. Is that really all I did? Even I can't imagine wasting that
much time. But it's true. Thinking a lot about Tim and my
Mother. Why all the drama? It really is a pain in the ass for me
to have to deal with my physical health and their mental health.
Why can't they get it together themselves. I spend so much time
on personal maintenance, why can't they channel a little? Have
to go download Sheree's pictures of me and my new haircut.

5/10/95 Really tired eyes. Short of breath. Heart palpitations on
the way home from Debbie's. Maybe I'll have a heart attack and
that will be that. Sheree blows her nose. Honk! Letterman. Did
nothing else today. Sat around while Carl cleaned up the joint.
Thinking a lot about Tim and how I don't deserve his wrath.
Mom, why doesn't she stand up for herself, stop playing games
and get on with her life. Fuck her kids. John—just an idiot. I
want to write letters to all of them, but it would all backfire in
my face. Let me die in peace, I'm fond of thinking. But I just
keep on thinking, not dying. Better start doing something while
I'm still here. If I could only keep my eyes open.

5/11/95 Trying to set up the small video camera to tape myself sleeping and masturbating and whatever, but I had a huge coughing fit and I couldn't find the video cable I needed and I didn't want to go upstairs again so I said to myself (and Kirby in space) fuck it, some other time. Tonight would have been good since Sheree's out "camping" in the desert at the Casa del Zoro. Would have been a good night for sex, too, some auto-erotic something or other, some shit eating would have hit the spot. But I'm wheezy and exhausted, not up to speed like last week. Distracted by family shit too in the back of my head. Tim and Mom and John. Dummies. I thought they were all supposed to help me? It winds up I can't say boo to any of them. Went to Social Security today. Thought it was going to be bad, but they're just going to cut 10% out of my check each month to make up for the money I earned on *The New Age*. I could fight it, but it's not worth it. Megan called tonight. Said she missed us, but then she asked a favor. She wants to copy a video tape for a grant she and Amy are writing. Oh, yeah, but she misses us. Well I don't miss her, or any one else. Just my dick, whom I'm going to visit just as soon as I turn off this computer.

5/12/95 I can't breathe. I look over at the cage in the corner of our bedroom and I feel a stirring in my balls. I want to be in there. I want to be fucked in the ass. I want to put alligator clips on my dick and take it. I want a lot of things, but all I'm doing is sleeping and sweating and watching tv. Morning and night. Should do more work on the computer. Should copy the Shiffler tapes. Should write letters. Should do work. Should live my life before it's over, but I can't breathe. Boiling water is a bitch. Anything that requires my body off the couch is a bitch. So I'm bitching. And people keep wanting stuff from me, and I feel guilty about not doing it for them. But I feel used too. And I bitch about it. Stupid paragraph for CF newsletter. It was Barbara's fault in the first place for screwing up the tape of our original interview in NY, which I was kind enough to grant. Now I'm supposed to save her neck by writing the damn article for her. She keeps saying "I hate to bother you." And I respond in my stupid way, "Don't worry about it. Bother away!" So I'm bothered. Another show that sounds stupid to me: *This/Ability*. Handicapped art. I don't want to be apart of that. So I ignore the first letter, and now they're bugging me again, and I don't want any part of it, but I feel guilty, so I'm still avoiding them. *This/Ability*. Fuck this ability.

Sheree's back. Letterman. Bed. Sleep.

5/13/95 In bed now, after sleeping all day on the couch. Sheree's at a party at Phil and LR's. I feel alone and stupid for not going, but it's better than feeling alone and stupid there, surrounded by a bunch of people I can't wait to get away from. They're all nice people, and maybe I feel guilty about being such an asshole, but I can't stand the boredom anymore. I'm tired. I have a headache. And it's a major effort to breathe, no matter what I do. So I stay home. More tv and more tv. Gotta start doing something. Bob's in Toyland. Ideas for a new show and new work, but do I have the steam? Talked to Mom today. She got the flowers I sent for Mother's Day. Talked mostly about Tim and John, and how I hoped she would get into therapy. She won't, no matter what she says. Oh, my aching head. Penis time.

5/14/95 I had a great hard-on, but now it's gone. Now that I'm writing and not masturbating, it's coming back. That fucker. I was sound asleep, several times. Sheree and I went to bed early, tuckered out after Mother's Day lunch at Barney's in Beverly Hills w/ Murray, Jenny, Richard and Ted, Molly and Eric. A worm crawling along the rim of my plate after an incredible dish of sturgeon got everyone grossed out and me a free lunch. Came home and finished editing performance tape for Liz Young. Another obligation I shouldn't have to have anything to do with, but I like Liz, and I tried to keep the work down to a minimum. Not so with these other projects that aren't mine and I don't even like to begin with but somehow feel guilty about because I'm ignoring them in favor of lying on the couch, sweating, watching tv and sleeping. The guilt is keeping me from doing what I want to do, like play with Photoshop or Premiere on the computer—my own projects—but I can't do it because I feel I have to respond in some way to this backlog of shit I never asked for and in fact tried to avoid in the first place. Oh, shit, where's a good hard-on when you need one? I go to bed early, around 9:30, and fall asleep watching a tape of X-Files with Sheree, but I wake up as she's video taping me. I make my penis talk for the camera, drunken bar penis. "All right, all right, I'm comin' goddamn you, you prick." Then it's sleep, cough, wake up; sleep, cough, wake up, until now, where it's 2:30 am, Sheree's snoring and I can't stop her, even if I shake her, even if I pinch her nose. So it's ear plugs in, which makes it impossible to hear "Perry Mason" on tv. Before Sheree plunged into the sawmill, earlier on, after my little penis show, she wanted me to suck her nipple while she masturbated with the vibrator. Not that I didn't want to, but I was still tired and ready to go back to sleep, and it usually takes her such a long time to come (we Paxil pals), that I just didn't want to get involved, but it would have been awful to deny her, so I went forth and commenced my sucking. I felt just like I did earlier this afternoon when I went out to the car to wait for her while she shopped at Barney's after lunch. I was too out of breath to walk around, so I sat in the car listening to the radio and waited for her to finish, knowing full well it could take forever. But lo and behold she came out relatively quickly, and what do you know, she came fast too, with a nice little shudder of completion, and before we knew it were both fast asleep, until now, for me anyway. Some weird dream I had, too. I had a pet parakeet, maybe two of them. I kept trying to play with it in its cage: giving it food, toys, playing with it with my hand. But somehow I was fucking it up. Sometimes the cage was a plastic bag, and I tried to shift the bird around so it could breathe. At some point the cage was like an oven, and I could see the parakeet getting singed and burnt, but it was too hot to put my hand in. Finally I managed to coax him out. He was alive still, but kind of crispy. One of his feet was melted. When I put him back in his cage I could see that he wasn't going to live. He was tiny and stiff. I felt guilty. I thought, since this was the second bird in one day that I had killed, did I do it on purpose, under the guise of "play?" Then I woke up and wrote all this stuff. Back to sleep, and maybe a hard-on if I'm lucky. And look, another *Perry Mason* episode that I won't be able to hear.

5/15/95 The bed. The snoring. The typing. The day. Canceled Obler because I wasn't breathing well and it was raining and I was exhausted as usual. I'm wasting a lot of time when I could be more productive, but I'm tired, and my eyes itch, and I don't want to do much—I mean I want to do work, but it's hard to get off the cough, to make the calls, to start the computer, to think the thoughts, to put it all down. And forget going anywhere. But I did drive Sheree to the photo place so she could get prints made for her UCI show this Saturday: dead mom and two sick significant others. And after a couple of hours of drenching my little couch pillow with head sweat I went to the storage place with Kirby to find the *Visible Man* for video close-ups later this week. Somewhat productive, huh? Sex on tv. Oh boy.

5/17/95 Finally in bed. Finally writing, if that's what you call it. Skipped writing yesterday cause my eyes were bulging after working with Sheree on her piss video for her opening this weekend. It's only 10 minutes long, but video is always a chore, and it always makes me irritable, especially when I'm working with Sheree, cause there's so much of it she doesn't understand cause she never has any hand's-on experience with the damn stuff cause she's always having me do everything and I don't understand much of it either, but I tinker, and you can't teach tinkering, so I get annoyed and a little irritable, but not as bad as I used to get, and today we finished up a nice little video, one that I don't quite get, but it's Sheree's piece, her vision, her "Wet Dream." Women pissing into each other's mouths—hot, yes, but is it art? I said to Kirby tonight that maybe that *is* Sheree's art: the presentation of these weird things to an unsuspecting crowd. It's the crowd that matters, to hell with art. Speaking of art, and speaking of Kirby, he's coming over again tomorrow morning to shoot the *Visible Man* close-ups. Getting geared up again to finish the documentary. Things he wants me to do: write an obituary; climb up several flights of stairs; force feeding party; find love letters to Sheree; look through old journals; track down *Wall of Pain* photos; and much much more. It's all I can do to turn on the television. And speaking of the documentary—Tim called yesterday, and we sort of had it out over the weirdness with Mom last week. He was pretty defensive and called me superior and accused me of calling *him* and criticizing *him*, when I had to remind him, ever so gently, that it was *he* who called *me*. How could I not be superior after that? I had to really put the breaks on my critical faculties when he started talking about how hurt his "inner child" still was after all these years. I ended it by saying I cared about how he felt, that I didn't want to lose the closeness I thought we had gained over the years, and that I hoped he would call me and talk to me about his feelings. He sort of grumbled something and said good bye, but I'm afraid he's going to steer clear of me for awhile and that make me feel bad. My mood definitely soured since this thing with Mom and Tim, which has probably added to my current irritability.

5/18/95 Oxygen mask is noisy and stupid looking, but I think I sleep more soundly, deeper anyway. But is it turned up too high? Don't know. Not going up stairs to change it. Too lazy. Lazy all the time. Out of breath and lazy. Kirby was over this morning to video the *Visible Man*, but it wasn't working right and I had to keep performing minor surgery on it, so we didn't get much done. Tomorrow. 9 am. Maybe one of these days I'll take a shower or a bath and wash my hair and shave or brush my teeth. But I don't give a fuck. Do I sound depressed? I've been bugged lately, but not depressed. Too cold in the morning, and too tired at night for the work of getting cleaned up. So I push my hair around and run a brush across my teeth and call it a day. And now a night. Tonight's tv shows on tape. Snoring soon. Big hardons in the morning, but they deflate on contact.

5/19/95 Laptop open and earplugs in. Might as well write cause I can't hear the tv, not unless I want to listen to Sheree's snoring as well. It seems like it's getting louder and louder. So I'm deaf at night. Need closed-caption tv. Fuck it, that's all I do is watch tv. I have all these great ideas but no energy to carry them through. I love sitting on the couch or lying here in bed at night watching tv. I love sleeping. I hate going out of the house. Don't give a shit about the phone. But why hasn't my mother called me? She's probably wondering why I haven't called her. Always have to call her. But I've been sleeping. Or working with Kirby. Finally shot the *Visible Man* close ups today. That's all I did. Played Jeopardy on the computer. Slept.

5/20/95 The phrase for today is: "Bend over backwards." As in: "We bent over backwards for you kids." "You could have bent over backwards to help us a little bit." It seems to me that everyone in my family has bent so far over backwards that they've completely snapped. I finally called Mom this morning and she started in crying about Tim and that whole fucking weekend, how I was part of it too. Who, me? "Well you could have bent over backwards a little bit. You could have pretended." (Pretended to like her friends, who were a bunch of fucking bores, twice our age, who had nothing in common with us, and were admittedly, as my mother says, straight-laced.) So we went to a movie, so what? She's a constant victim. I thought everyone was supposed to be there for me? Are they there to drive me crazy? I hope they all work it out before I check out. Too tired now to work it out here. Sheree had her opening tonight. Pissed that her pictures (Dan, me, and her mother) weren't lighted properly. Then she showed her piss video to a drop-jawed PC crowd. What a sight. A Sheree shower. I was afraid that she'd be depressed too over the reaction, but she got some good feedback, and she took the negative for what it was worth. Now we're both here in bed watching that ever glorious television.

5/21/95 Leaning back in bed. Computer on my lap, resting on my dick. Nothing good coming out of the computer or my dick. No great words of wisdom today. No accomplishments other than a couple of rounds of Jeopardy, a nap on the couch. Went to Bruce Yonomoto's birthday party which we weren't really invited to, but Rita and Kirby were, so we went. Pleasant time by one and all. Sheree stoned and drunk. Me a nervous nelly. People continually ask me how I'm doing. They say I look good. I try not to be too positive, or too negative. I'm somewhere in the middle. Yeah, I look ok. I am ok, as long as I don't do anything, or move too fast. But anything beyond sitting on the couch is a stretch for me. In spite of it all, and in spite of my family going bonkers on me, my mood is relatively up. I've been a little more cranky, a little more annoyed around Sheree, but I'm still doing fairly well upstairs. I see Obler tomorrow when I can spill all. Whine whine whine.

5/22/95 Bed. Little camera on for Kirby. Sheree high as hell beside me. Said there was a present for me downstairs. I knew it was shit. She only does shit stuff when she's stoned. I didn't want to eat it, and thankfully she didn't push it. Just now she wanted to drip hot wax on me, but I said no to that too. Not when she's stoned. Makes me too nervous. And my SM mode which I felt so great about a few weeks ago, is gone again. I'm a wimp again. Not feeling well, that has something to do with it. Short of breath, thick phlegm, tired as hell. And I'm a wimp. Saw Obler today. Started going on and on about my mother and Tim and John and I felt like a mush mouth, even thought Obler was falling asleep. Truth is there's not a fucking thing I can do about their problems. I'm as loving and as supportive as I can be. The rest they have to take care of themselves. I don't know if it's the Zoloft or what, but some other time I would have been obsessed with their depression and their anger, taking it on as my own, weeping little tears over it, working desperately to change things somehow. Maybe it's therapy. Maybe it's drugs. Maybe it's my own death rattle keeping me preoccupied, but I'm just not that worked up about it. I'm sad for them. I want them to get their shit together—I'm starting to bore myself again. Fuck it.

5/24/95 Too tired last night to write, and slept almost all day today. Heavy flu-like sleep. Short of breath. Feel better now that I'm here in bed. Itchy face, need to shave. It's past 11:00 and Sheree's still not back from school. That's pretty late. When do I start worrying? When do I stop? When do I start writing? Kirby wants me to write my obituary for the film. I should write a bunch of them, since I have no idea how I'll die. Well, I have a pretty good idea, but one ever knows. I don't know how I feel these days. Bad. Not horrible, but not great. Not depressed, but not happy. Just alive. Just living. Barely breathing. Again, I'm boring myself. Is that the sound of the garage door? Sheree? Yes. My ears perk up. My tail wags.

5/25/95 Letterman. Earplugs. Boredom. And more bad writing. I'm just so lethargic, day and night. Sleep all day on the couch. Come down to bed at night, write some shit here about the nothing I do all day, and then it's off to sleep. Blah. I want to be involved in something but I'm out of breath when I do anything, or when I even think of doing anything. It's easier to go to sleep. And I like the way it feels to sleep. I like typing here in bed with the television on. I like touching my balls when I'm done and surfing the channels. Too bad there's nothing good on, but I like it anyway. It would be better to read something, and I will, I will, but not just yet. Tomorrow is another day. If only I was another writer.

5/26/95 Lying back here in bed, computer on my lap, penis poking over the keyboard. Actually did a little work tonight on the confetti casket photos. Need to step it up, get something done. Nothing on my brain but a pounding headache inside. Air sucked in and blown out. Phlegm all over the god damned place. Bloody, crusty, sore nose. I'd like to be brilliant. But I'm just sitting here staring at my dick. Watching tv. Off of it and out of it.

5/27/95 High tech again in bed. Wireless headphones hooked up to the tv so I can plug in my earplugs and still hear the tv while

Sheree snores blissfully through the night without me to poke her and prod her and beg her to turn over so I can hear Letterman or whatever crap is on without that sawing noise that's like poison ivy to my brain. I'm glad she won't be bugging me, but mostly I'm glad I don't have to bug her. Babble babble babble. Actually worked on the computer today, and didn't sleep on the couch. Worked on designing videotape labels. Scanned in and cropped photos for the confetti casket. It's looking great. It gives me chills to look at all those photographs of me, all different times, different poses, different me's, all in rows of half inch squares. It's dazzling. I know some people will look at this as the ultimate in narcissism, but as I know my life is getting shorter I want to gather it all together in the form of these photographs — all the photographs — that have ever been taken of me. It feels good to be working on this. It's going to be great — if only somebody would fucking buy something.

5/28/95 Very productive day of scanning and cropping photos for the confetti casket. Have to figure how to get them printed and cut. Don't know what else I did today. Obsessed with my own face and its place in history. Now it's in bed watching the McMartin movie. Scary what they can do to people. Are they doing it right now to OJ? Don't think so, but what did I think about the McMartin's back then? Don't remember. I think that I was jealous that I didn't get to go to a school like that when I was a kid.

5/29/95 I'm obsessed with the computer. Had to stop scanning and cropping today, first to go to Debbie's, and then because we had a barbeque here at the condo complex. Sheree invited Murray and Evelyn, Ted and Richard, Jennifer, Stephenie, Molly, and Ed Smith showed up too. I doubted everyone would mix well with the neighbors (because I don't) but it was a nice day. I stayed inside most of the time because my breathing was the shits, and I can't stand trying to talk to people, and at the same time eat and breathe. So I hung out in the house, playing

Jeopardy on the computer. Had to stop scanning cause I didn't think everyone wanted to see hundreds of images of my dick. I like it though, maybe a little too much. I realized today that making collages in puberty I always looked through magazines for pictures of tits, assses, hot-looking women. No cunts—I was too chicken to be that blatant. Everything I did had to be suppressed somehow. Probably made the work better. But now I'm just as turned on by the sight of me, my own dick, my ass (skinny as it is) and my piss, shit, or whatever. I get hard looking at myself. Can you believe it? Mr. Auto Erotic. I'm not in love with myself. And it's not that I think that I'm all that great, it's just that I see my body for the sexual history it contains—a sexual map—and it gets me going. And then I think about the possibilities, where I want to go, like lately I'm thinking about cutting my testicles off before I die—right before I die, when I'm done with them and don't need them anymore—I want to cut them off myself and give them to Sheree to remember me by, and to video the whole thing, of course, and maybe charge money for the whole final performance—but what will I need with money? Ok, fuck the money idea, what am I, crazy? I just want to cut my fucking balls off and that's that.

5/30/95 Saw Riker today. He said I looked good. "Must be the haircut," he said. I tried to tell him that I was slowly starting downhill again. Feeling like shit whenever I try to do anything, but there's not much to do about it. It's CF. I've got several strains of pseudomonis, but what am I going to do about it unless I want to go back into the hospital and start the IV again. Not ready for that. Too much to do, or try to do, on the outside. Keep going on the confetti. Get tapes ready for Shiffler. Try to get some more of this art stuff moving. Sheree's depressed again, first time in a long time, mostly about art. I tell her it's not unusual to have doubts about your work, it's part of the process. I think something else is going on. Menopause. She's all sweaty and clammy and tossing and turning in bed all night. Whining and moaning. I like squeezing her big butt. I should go down on her or something. But any kind of sex is too much of an effort, especially where I have to lie down and go down and not come up for air. I panic when I think of it. It's not sex I'm afraid of, it's breathing. I think of sexual activity the way I think of walking up the stairs: I'll go out of my way to avoid it. Except I don't miss walking up the stairs.

5/31/95 Sheree's all over the bed, kicking my computer. She wants to read what I've been writing. What have I been writing? Just stuff. Not into it now. Distracted by the tv, the HBO McMartin movie. Keep seeing bits and pieces of it. Scary stuff. Heavy handed prosecution and even heavier-handed film makers. But I don't care about all that. This is where I came in, any who. More scanning and cropping today. Typed resume for Sheree before she went to school. She's been depressed about her art career and her work, but she seems better tonight. I'm not wildly enthusiastic about the art biz either. After New York's big splash we're just treading water. No gallery. No more collectors. Sold $4000 worth of something or other in Geneva. That's not bad. But in the meantime what about that big casket in the garage? And the alphabet block wall? And now this new confetti idea, and don't forget the punching bags. I'm going to finish all these things if it's the last thing I do—and it probably will be—but who's interested in it but me? Don't know. I'll just have to be enough.

June, 1995

6/1/95 Feel awful. Neck ache. Headache. Sore eyes. Chest pain. Difficulty breathing. These are a few of my favorite things. Where'd the day go? Worked on the computer, but mostly on stuff for Sheree before she went to school. Feeling really greedy with my time. Don't even want to take the time to talk to people on the phone. Mark Robin is coming tomorrow. Wants to spend the whole day with us. Of course we will, but I just want to work on my stuff and time with him (or anyone) is time away from my stuff. But I'm too nice a guy to say no.

6/2/95 Plagued with headaches. Why not start with what I do best—complaining. Mark's visit was pleasant. Entertained Andrew with our toy box and our talking toy mina bird. Shy at first, but giggles soon enough. Saw Stuart Boone too. Went to Debbie's. Sheree went to the west side for dinner with Murray and the rest. Falling aslee...

6/3/95 In considerable pain. Eyes feel like they're bugging out of my head. Neck muscles are so tight they're strangling me. And my temples and forehead are banging like a drum. Vicodin doesn't help much. Wish I could get something stronger, like Demerol. It's hard to do work with all this discomfort. What kind of work would I do on Demerol? Who cares? Had dinner at Thai Dishes with Mark and Stuart and Debbie, along with their respective two year olds, Emily and Andrew. Good to see them all again but I couldn't wait to get home to my Vicodin and my nakedness and my computer and my television. Sheree's upstairs watching Michael Tolkin's *The Rapture*. She says she's watching it, but when I was up there she kept fading out and breathing in that whistling snore that annoys me so. And I was falling asleep too. Now that I'm down here in bed she's probably wide awake up there.

6/4/95 Just knocked Sheree's video camera off the dresser and onto the floor. Crash! Snapped a cable but the camera's ok. "Be careful with my camera, honey." "I didn't do it on purpose." "Now you sound like Matthew." "Now you sound just as stupid as you did when you were talking to Matthew. Sometimes there *are* such things as accidents." Anyway, nothing's broken. Finally set up the video camera to tape myself sleeping for Kirby. It's taping now, even as we speak, and the tv blares on with another documentary, not about me, but Sonny Liston. Before that we caught the latest *Gutter Vision* with a performance by the late non-great GG Allyn, fellow naked performance artist, fellow shit-eater. But what a tiny penis he had. No wonder he shot himself. Still fucked up with headaches, neck aches and the like. And both Sheree and I have awful dry, bloody, crusty noses. I thought mine was from the oxygen, but Sheree's got it too. Snot funny. But the big news today is I think I tracked down the episode of the old Steve Allen show that I was on when I was a kid. December 11, 1962. I hope that's the one. Kirby and I are going to the film archives this week and check out the tape. Exciting. I've been looking for this tape for twenty years.

6/5/95 Fun and frustration with the computer. First, I added some photographs to the January journal, which I just finished transcribing last night. But mostly the computer's given me nothing but trouble today. I was trying to do more scanning and cropping but the damn thing kept bombing and freezing and crashing. There are a few things I can try tomorrow, but I'm not sure what's going on. We're taking it in to the shop anyway to add a couple of gigabytes, so maybe Les can fix whatever's wrong. I sound like a real computer geek, I know, but all my projects are on it now. I'd rather be in front of the computer than anywhere else. Something to do with getting my life in order. My command post. A place where I can get a lot done without doing a lot (physically). I get depressed when it starts giving me trouble. The waste of time. The confusion. The disarray. My life, which is all computerized and digitized by now, feels like it's crashing around me when the system dies. A little melodramatic, yeah, but I'm only human.

6/6/95 Mr. Sore Nose. And headaches too. Should invent a software to catalogue all my complaints. There's lots of them these days. And the computer's still flipping out on me. I worked with it most of the day, but then tonight it started crashing and bombing all over the place. So fuck it, now I'm down here on the lap top which never lets me down, because I mainly just write on it. But just now I discovered I've got the software to make any text talk, not just the "Pop Psychologist" game I was playing with a while ago. So I took last night's entry and had the computer read it back to me and it sounded great. Sad. The electronic voice reading my text was very moving. Something about me being absent from it all, especially since the last entry was about becoming computerized to begin with. Hmmm. This could lead to something.   Sheree's upstairs doing another jigsaw puzzle. I wish she'd come down here

6/7/95 Sitting back in bed, computer on pillow/ on lap/ on dick position. Can hardly keep my eyes open. Quadra in shop getting more gigs. Just dozed off. Maybe later…

6/8/95 Going back into the hospital. Phlegm is really dark, really thick and oh so plentiful. Can't breathe. Terrible headaches. Pain in my right sinus, behind my eye and all the way down into the root of my tooth. Is is a toothache? Keep banking on the hope that my teeth won't give out before my lungs do. Don't need all that dentist shit. Went to Jim Shaw's book signing tonight, despite my feeling lousy. Sheree's push. Stoned push. Same as trying to push me into recording some workshop bullshit for the reading I had to cancel out on at Beyond Baroque tomorrow. It's not worth the energy to put the five minutes together just to remind people that I'm not there because I'm in the hospital. They don't need to hear all that crap again. I'm exhausted. Tried to work with the computer a little after getting it back from Les, but it's still acting weird, crashing and stuff in Photoshop. Shit. Sheree freaks out about it. "It's the nature of computers," I say, and keep saying. But she doesn't hear it. She doesn't get it.

6/9/95 After all the complaining, of course I'm in the hospital. Headaches, chest aches, phlegm and all the rest of the shit, the boring shit, my mean mantra. Can I get some other kind of pain relievers maybe, like Demerol or morphine? Don't know if I really need something that heavy, the pain's not excruciating, it's just constant and annoying, to say the least. But why shouldn't I be able to zone out a little? Where am I going? What else do I have to do? I just checked some previous entries in the journal, and lo and behold it was exactly two months ago I was in here last. That's my schedule, every two months in, two weeks of IV on the outside, a few weeks of feeling energetic, sexy even, and then the gradual slide back into the mucus pit. When I get this bad I can't help but worry that I'm getting close to the end. But each time it seems to be two steps closer, and then after the antibiotics, rest and extra calories, it's two and a half steps back again. And then the process starts all over. That's why I don't fight about coming into the hospital so much. I think this routine is what's keeping me alive and able to do at least some of what I want to do when I'm well.

6/10/95 What are the highlights of Saturday in the hospital? Bloody phlegm. The usual aches and pains. The usual drugs. Three different IV antibiotics. Lots of sleeping. Transcribing here in the computer. Playing Jeopardy. Sheree, Ed, Mom and

Dad on the phone. Where's Tim? Is that it? Am I personae non grata now because I had the nerve to criticize him? There are so many people who seem to have cut me off. Some with elaborate and phony fights like David. Most just stop calling. Dennis. But I don't really care. I don't have the energy to give to these people anyway. It's the ones who want to fight with me like Tim and David. They piss me off. The last (and only) time David and I talked about this shit and I got pissed he said, "See, I knew you'd be defensive." Well damn right, and I'm sick of defending myself. So I was a bossy big brother. So I'm sometimes self-absorbed in this difficult time of my life. Get on my train or fuck off. I can't carry you. The ruminations of the bedridden. Here lies Bob Flanagan. Bob Flanagan: Dead at? Kirby wants me to write an obituary for the Bobumentary. "Bob's Dead." There you go.

6/11/95 Hospital. Nothing on television. Been reading the new *Grand Street* that Sheree brought today—distracted from this writing by the stupid tv. Dumb ass talk show with some teenage girl telling her parents that she dates black men. The whole show's about revealing secrets on the air. I think they're all a bunch of phonies and most of this shit is prefabricated. But what do I care? I should turn the fucker off, but I won't, and that's my dirty little secret. "Raped her, tortured her, mutilated and killed her, with her hands tied behind her back." Different channel. Different show. Now we're talking. The theme of the new *Grand Street* is "Fetishes," and it has a great full color spread on *Visiting Hours*. Maybe this will pique some new interest in our stuff and we can sell some more of it, especially the coffin and the blocks. Stopped to talk to Sheree on the phone. Tried to interest her in this great show on PBS about toads. Beautifully shot. "All right," she says. "I'll go watch toads." And so will I.

6/12/95 Vicodin kicking in. Not much of a kick anymore. More like a tap on the shoulder. And when I turn around there ain't nobody there. And then the headache's back. Who's this nurse I've got tonight? Never saw a porta cath before? I hate new nurses that don't know me at night. I want *them* taking care of *me*, not me them. What a whiner. Looks like I'll be here till next Monday. Sheree none too happy bout that, but that's the way it goes. Riker's going to be gone from Wednesday through Friday, so I can't go home then. So it's on to Monday. What if I just wrote wrote wrote? Naw naw naw. Almost finished transcribing this year's written journal, up to the point where I started using this here laptop with a lip. It's got a lip cause it talks back to me, it reads my stuff in this real sad disembodied voice that I find quite compelling. This is nuts, but it reminds me of when I was a kid and used to have puppets with me to keep me company in the hospital. Now instead of making a puppet talk I can make this machine my alter ego. Could have been a good Groundlings skit. "Bob and Mac." I think my Vicodin wave has passed. I prayed for Demerol, not because I needed it, but my body remembers it when I'm in here, and it just feels so fucking good, for a few minutes anyway, but no real justification for it. I keep looking for one, but no. I am feeling better. Breathing better, but I'm not doing anything but sitting here in bed. I'm remarkably well-adjusted to being here. Sheree wants me home. She sounded very lonely on the phone. It's harder on her than it is on me, it always will be. I'm the center of attention, even at the worst of it. But for her, she'll always be alone. I just called her back and had the computer say, "I forgot to tell you I love you." And I do. (And if you're reading this, Sheree, don't forget it.)

6/13/95 Computer on my pillow. Pillow sandwich between my dick and my computer. Does I still has a dick? More aches and pains from the aches and pains ward. No Demerol. Some Vicodin. The names of these drugs are capitalized as if they were gods. St. Vicodin. Lord Demerol. Our Lady of Cephtazidime. Let's not forget the great and powerful Zoloft, son of Prozac. Enough of that. Supposed to try this stupid bipap thing again tonight. A respirator designed for snorers, but it's supposed to give me some relief while I breathe during the night, and maybe alleviate some of the headaches and pain the next day. I'd rather have Demerol. Richard, one of the kids I know from camp, stopped in to say hi. He gets Demerol. What about me? He has a G tube in his stomach, I don't. But I can dream, can't I. So tonight I wear this stupid jock strap kind of thing on my face to see if it gives my lungs a break. It may make the headaches worse because it forces air into the sinuses. Maybe then I'll get some Demerol.

6/14/95 Don't get it. Sheree and Scott came by to visit a few hours ago, Sheree bouncing off the walls of course. They stayed for about fifteen minutes and then went for something to eat, and I haven't heard from them since. She said she was coming back, so what gives? So I start worrying. Carjacked? Arrested? Accident? Stoned—that's for sure, and that means anything's possible. Visiting hours are long over and security's tight around here, so I don't know when I'll hear from them. Meanwhile my head is splitting open. The bipap took the dull ache I had and honed it into a burning hot poker stabbing me right behind the eyes. And Riker won't give me any Demerol. Not good for my CO_2. But what about the discomfort? And where the hell is Sheree? Probably out farting around with Scott, and will most likely wander in by 10:00, in time to watch the Michael Jackson interview. Not into writing. Hot and bothered. Distracted. Ed Smith called but I didn't want to talk. Left a messaage for Amy. What's with her? More abandonment? I'm abandoning this. More on the bicrap tonight. Riker gone for two days. Definitely no hope for Demerol now.

6/15/95 Tonight's notes, before I slip off into my pharmaceutical soup. No Demerol, but Riker's alternate, Dr. Libby Libby Libby, prescribed Percocet, to melt the headaches—which are real, make no mistake about it. I'm not just looking for a cheap buzz. I want relief. The Percocet works a bit I spose, but the "buzz" aspects of Demerol are sorely missed. And, speaking of sorely missed, Sheree came by again today. Some mysterious trip down here to Long Beach to buy some mysterious thing for me, but she's mum and cagey about the whole thing, so I don't know. I was right about last night. She and Scott showed up just in time to watch the ridiculous Michael Jackson and Lisa Marie Presley "interview." Just took a shit break, even though the toilet won't flush. Better report it. My dick's burning. Better report it. This stuff sucks. Report it. Gonna stop soon, lie back, watch the stupid TV. Boring Letterman. No bicrap tonight, makes the headaches worse. Sleep better, but not worth the hassle. Although I was looking forward to incorporating the face mask into a leather hood, so at least the humiliation of it all would have a more erotic component, and I wouldn't look so much like a guy wearing a jock strap on his head all night.

6/16/95 A full week here in the hospital. Breathing is better. Still heaving up this dark green phlegm pudding. Headaches more under control with Percocet. It's got a nice rubbery effect to it, for a brief time, anyway. Weird rainy day. What did I do all day? No shower or teeth brushing or gown changing for me. Just flat on my back. Breakfast, Lunch, Dinner, Percocet. Jeopardy on the computer. Amy on the phone. Bob and Dixie on the phone. Sheree on the phone. Wild guess that the mysterious item she came down here to buy yesterday was a "pee boy" fountain for her garden. She got pissed off that I got it right. I can't help it if I'm so smart. Hey, where's my Percocet. Jerk is set on Percocet. Sometimes the writing has a spark to it, and sometimes it's just crapola like this. OK. "The nurse just brought me my Percocet. I'm going to fold up this laptop. Turn the lights off. Lie back and watch *Cops*, and Letterman, and then I'm going to melt away into the night.

6/17/95 Long dull day. Sleepy from Percocet. Headaches in between. Sheree on the phone. Ed on the phone. Amy on the phone. Crabb on the phone. Nothing to say to Ed and Amy. Always laugh when I'm talking to Bob. Laughing about old pictures of me and what a jerk I was. And why didn't anyone stop me. And what about now? Probably still a jerk. Watching this dumb TV. Craving my dumb drugs. Still won't give me Demerol. And what would I do if I had it? I can't be doped up all the time. So we're going to do a CAT scan and sinus xray to see what's inside my head that's pounding to get out… stop now for a breathing treatment… breathing treatment done. Headache back. Percocet swallowed. Waiting for the kick, the nudge. Tonight's nurse is very tall and smily. Looks like Paula Prentiss or Geena Davis. A pleasing pill passer.

6/18/95 All of it is in every bit of it. Got it? What I got is gunk in my sinuses again. CAT scan this morning. Supposed to go home tomorrow, but not sure now with all this crap in my head what they want to do about it. More surgery? Didn't help last time. Sheree's depressed at the thought of me not coming home. But I think she'd be depressed even if I were coming home. It's her time. No Paxil for awhile. Weird ovulations. We've discovered a part of ourselves that is beyond change. 10:00. Getting very sleepy again. Percocet time, almost. Headache just starting. I may get Demerol after all if I have to stay for this crappy surgery. I have no idea what to write. No strong streak of intellectual curiosity here. New wave quotes lifted from PBS. Body, Mind and Soul. Got a sandwich here I should eat, and some milk to drink, and then some drugs to take. Dupac Chopra? PBS Guru. Nothing else on TV, Sunday night in the hospital. PBS pledge drive.

6/19/95 Home, ensconced in my spot on the bed after dozing on the couch after, what else, doing my drugs—anti-antibiotics. Discombobulated as always when I first come home. And I'm sorry to say the headache is much worse and I didn't ask for Percocet to take home with me because I didn't want to feel dopey all the time, but what's the difference with this water balloon head that feels like it's about to explode? More: I sleep for only an hour or so and then wake up, witness to a murder. Is that Sheree fighting with some guy and choking him? I wake up and the first thing I see is some woman fighting with some guy. The room is dark but I see them struggling in a brightly lit window.

Am I looking at Sheree in the bathroom? Am I really seeing her fighting with some guy? I think I even called out her name. And then I saw that what I was looking at was the reflection of the television in the glass door. There was a woman fighting with some guy but it was only a movie, only a movie. But this headache is real. I'm sick of typing the words "headache." Repetitive and boring. Tired again. Back to sleep. Back to the "window."

6/20/95 Transfixed by the sight of a guy tied to a bed by three women. HBO movie called *All Tied Up*. Those were the days. Headaches bad again today, and it looks like my feet are swelling up. What's the deal? Saw Debbie tonight, and she was crying and talking a lot about Shawnee. Anniversary her wedding and her death. She's afraid of something happening to me, but nothing ever happens to me anymore. This bondage guy did something to one of these women, so now it's payback time. I miss payback time. Now it's late, real late. The guy's been cut free. They led us on to think they were going to cut his balls off or something, but no, they just cut him loose. The movies. In real life I'm tied to oxygen tubes and IV lines and earplugs and pain pills and steroids and bronchial dialators and television and pictures of myself and the sound of my own voice and sleep.

6/21/95 Late again. Down here in the dark, typing while the tv flickers, but the rush of air thundering through the confines Sheree's fleshy palette is the only sound I can hear, even with these wadded up bits of foam crammed into my oh so sensitive ear canals. Do these earplugs make my headaches worse? No. The headaches are just bad, period, no matter what. Just took three Vicodin. My eyes are killing me. There was something on the news about a new drug for migraines, but I fell asleep on the couch while doing my antibiotics and I missed it. I don't know what the drug is, and besides these aren't migraines. I don't know what they are, but I'm getting tired of writing about them and more tired of having them. They seem worse since I've been home. Sheree has headaches too. Is there something in the air here? Some weird chemical in our house? Some sort of gas? Don't know. Just trying to get work done in the midst of the stupor. Waited all day for the oxygen man to come, but he didn't. Sheree worked on her jigsaw puzzle. She wouldn't talk to Donna when she called, the way she hasn't talked to anybody lately. She says she's depressed. There's something that so sad about her working on those damn jigsaw puzzles. I got struck with a wave of sadness yesterday when I was teasing her, stealing one of her pieces, and pretending to hide it. But I told her right away where it was because for some reason I felt sorry for her. The puzzle seemed to matter so much to her. She seemed so vulnerable. I felt creepy stealing her pieces, even as a joke. So today when Donna called and the machine picked up, and Sheree wouldn't leave her puzzle to talk to her, I got pissed and declared into the void, "That's it! No more jigsaw puzzles." That's telling her. By the way, the Christians are after us again, using us as examples again of offensive art supported by the NEA. Got a call from Tosh at Beyond Baroque and Laura at the Lab (someone else whose call Sheree won't return because she has "nothing to say.") This time the Christians are upset because of my "cata-logue" of work wherein I have oral sex with myself (I wish), smear myself with feces (Swiss Miss chocolate pudding) and, worst of all, have a crown of thorns tattooed around my genitals and have the nerve to call it "He is Risen." Blasphemer! Too bad there's no more inquisition. Too bad there are no more lions.

6/23/95 Guess what? No headache. That's because I just took three Percocets. I was in agony last night and this morning. The Vicodin were no more effective than Vicks Cough Drops, and besides Riker hadn't yet called the pharmacy back to renew my prescription, so I called him and asked him to change it to Percocet since that worked so well in the hospital. We had to drive all the way down to Long Beach to pick it up because they wouldn't let him call it in, it being a narcotic and all. Terrible traffic due to a tanker truck that exploded on the freeway last night. But we got down there in good time, and it was not a moment too soon, because my head was exploding. And three and a half hours into the Percocet it starts hurting all over again. I can't keep taking drugs like this, but I'm sick of suffering. It's not the kind of suffering I like, and I can't ignore it or hypnotize myself into making it go away. As you can see it occupies a lot of my thinking. But I felt much better after the Percocet. Worked on the computer. Shaved Sheree's cunt and licked her clit, and sucked her nipple until she came. And come she did, all around the mountain. Maybe one of these days we'll actually fuck again. Falling asleep. That's why there was no writing last night. Sleep. It's so good.

6/24/95 Check in time, since I'm awake, sort of. Fell asleep on the couch, doing drugs. Sheree also asleep, on the couch, after an evening of art auction shmoozing at Santa Monica Museum of Art and dinner at Netty's with Rita. So we both wake up and make it down here to bed, but I wake up again with a stabber of a headache (there's that word again), but it's too soon for Percocet cause I took it the last time I woke up, two hours ago. Trying to be a responsible druggie. Spent the day on the computer, mostly. Put a Jeffrey Hunter Jesus head on my penis head with Photoshop. It really looks beautiful. My response to the Christian Action Network. "He is Risen." But I need to get back to sleep... just fell asleep with my fingers on the keys as I pondered my next sentence and tried to think back when the last Percocet wasdddddddd... those d's are my fingers passing out on the keyboard. I'm outta here.

6/25/95 I like the sight of Sheree's bald pussy. My handy work. I should ball that pussy. But I'm such a pussy myself, I'm always too tired or too short of breath or too something. But this morning I was a human Erector set with all the hard-ons I was getting. The slightest touch, and there it was. No coming though. Can't seem to manage that. But these are bonafide boners and they feel good. When all else fails at least I know the plumbing is still functional. Now all we need to do is stick it in and ride it around once in a while. But while I was waxing passionate over my pumped up prick, Sheree was deeply engrossed in her crossword puzzle and her Jumble Word. Too bad. Well, at least the flesh is willing. Must be the Percocet. I've been much more energetic lately, at least for an hour or so after taking it. Then it wears off and it's time to take it again. What's a nine letter word for "habit forming?"

6/26/95 Jam packed day today. Computer. Video. Therapy. Drugs. The highlight is, of course, the Steve Allen tape from 1962. The one with me on it. Sheree and I went to U-L-C-E-R to have a look, and wow! There I was, the "young man in the audience." Little squeaky voice: "Robert Flanagan." Collage I made for Steve Allen, still sticky with paint. "So, you want to be an artist when you grow up?" "No. I'm going to be a doctor." "Well, you know, you could be both." I couldn't believe I was finally watching this after 30 years. I'm amazed at how serious and articulate I was. And the art wasn't bad either. When Steve asked me what school I went to I told him I didn't go to school because I just got out of the hospital. And there's the cough, way back then, the prelude of so much more to come. It's all there: the art, the illness. It's going to blow this documentary out of the water... if we can get the rights. Saw Obler today, too, but not feeling bad about anything so we talked about art and Percocet. Uh oh, forgot to bring it down here to bed with me. What if I need it tonight? Hot tail it up stairs, that's what. *The Beast with Five Fingers* is on tv right now. Peter Lorre. Severed hand walking all over the place. One of our favorites as kids. And speaking of kids and blasts from the past, Mom sent me some old photos, some with me as a baby, one with Dad on the couch, holding me on his lap. I took a recent picture of me on a couch and spliced it in, sitting next to my dad and myself. It's almost a perfect match. I knew I wanted send him something for Father's Day, but this is turning out better than I expected. I'm definitely on a roll. Spent the past couple of hours scanning in and faxing out the Christian bullshit. Kirby's cousin is going to try and tape their "offensive" exhibition tomorrow. I'm tired now. Sheree's grinding away. Loudly! Even though I've got earplugs AND headphones AND Peter Lorre in my ears. It's 1:30 now. I've got to crawl off and get some sleep.

6/27/95 To break up the monotony I'm still upstairs, at the command post instead of in bed next to the snoring Sheree and the boring tv. Fell asleep on the couch again while doing antibiotics. Have to be up again in five hours to do them again, so do I go downstairs or do I stay up here? Life is tough. Hard to stay awake. Been here at the computer most of the day. Finished putting the final touches on the image of myself on the couch next to my dad and my infant self. Very eerie. I'm thrilled with myself. I got an idea for another Jesus print: the photo of me lying in the bathtub with a big hard-on and the head of my dick nestled comfortably into a pile of Sheree's shit heaped onto my abdomen. I'm going to Photoshop another movie Jesus head onto my penis head and call this one "Corpro Christi." I spent the whole morning and afternoon ruminating on this one, how to link Jesus Christ with this very hot photo of me and a pile of shit, and make it fit logically. Sheree dragged me out of the house to go with her to pick out a base for her "Pee Boy" fountain. Piss and shit seem to be a big theme with us. While she was writing out her check and placing her order I was sitting on a stone bench staring at terra cotta angels and thinking about Jesus and shit. "Corpus Christi," a place in Texas, but also "the body of Christ," kept going through my head: corpus Christi—coprophelia—corpus Christi—corporfelia. Then, back at home, it hits me: Corpus Christi: "Shit Christ." Again I'm thrilled with myself, and that's a good thing, because a lot of people are not going to be so thrilled.

6/28/95 Percocet Pete at 5:33 in the morning on Wednesday, June 28, 1995. So? Sheree kicks her feet and turns in her sleep, almost knocking Mac off the bed. Now she strokes my back. Better take an earplug out to see if she's talking to me. No. Dawn's early light illuminates the brazen Pee Boy outside our bedroom door. Wish it were me out there, stark naked in the morning chill, holding on to my alabaster penis.

6/29/95 Drugs done. Real tired. Three Stooges on tv. No sound cause Sheree says no, anything but the Three Stooges, so I turn the sound off but not the tv, not yet. Too tired to get up off my ass to change it. Too tired to write. Head hurts. Sweating. Out.

6/30/95 Sharp pains around the eyes. Black ants along the floor, up and down the walls, tracking across my computer cable, searching the trash for my discards, trying to get a mandible full of my fortifying phlegm. I heave the whole kit and caboodle of them out the door, into Sheree's garden. Tomorrow the trashcan will be a regular Uncle Milton's. Went to ULCER with Sheree and Kirby today to see the Steve Allen tape again and at least tape it off the television screen until we can obtain a copy of it. Kirby wanted to get some footage of me huffing and puffing and turning blue on the long walk from the car to the media center. He was hoping a few flights of stairs to turn me sufficiently blue for his opus, but we found a handicapped space so most of the walking was kept to a minimum, much to the consternation of Kirby.

7/1/95 The problem with writing at the end of the day is that it is often so far to the end there's nothing left. So here I am, Sunday morning, the second day of July, not the first, but writing about the first, since at six in the morning not enough has happened to punch these keys about. Sheree's still snoring, ear plugs, tv, blah blah blah. My blood specked phlegm. The pee boy in all his glory. Those pesky ants. My aching head. Percocet no longer the panacea it had promised to be. The headaches come back too quickly and too fiercely for any nonsense beyond the therapeutic. No more surfing the synapses. Have to go up and do my other drugs soon. Then the day really starts. Hope it's a better one than yesterday. Couldn't wake up yesterday. Can't stay awake now. "D's" fill he screen, but it's just my sleepy left fuck finger sleeping on its "D" key, not a poor grade. Although if you were to grade the day, that's the grade you'd give it.

7/2/95 The end of the second day, beginning of the next, and it's not much better than the last. Sheree moping around and giving me the silent treatment all day. She's depressed again. Out of the blue. I believe it's post pot and post Percocet enhanced. (that's the last time I let her have one of my Percocets). After pot and Percocet, throw in another "P": PARTY. There's no winning here. To go or not to go, it makes no difference. There are other people in the world gathering together, either right before our eyes, or conspiratorially behind our backs, and they are all having a great time, they are living THE life, they're doing it right, they're having fun, they're the ones who are famous, they're hot, they're in, they're not losers like us, they get invited to parties and we don't even though we're here, invited to the same party— forget it, they get invited to better parties because they're better people, and they have more fun, and we're just rubes. Leslie's the hottest thing in rubber since Trojans. That's what she is, the Trojan horse ambushing Sheree's emotions, and then Sheree dumps it all on me, and I could give a rat's ass about Leslie or Nan, or any of them. No matter how hot Sheree thinks they are, I find them pretentious and boring. She may be the Trojan horse where Sheree's concerned, but for me she's a one trick pony. The same rubber dress, the same patter, the same pseudo dominance/ pseudo submissive bull, the same one-ups-man-ship, I've seen it for ten years now and I'm not impressed. From a non-judgmen-tal point of view, I'm just not a voyeur: SM is boring. Unless you're the spanker or the spankee, or unless it's all new to you and you're seeing this shit for the first time, the most painful part of SM is having to watch the same people do the same thing year in and year out with no other context and no other meaning, no sense of humor, no originality, no art. Sorry, I'd rather stay home. But the whole point of this evening that makes me mad is that I wanted to go to the party this time. Sheree didn't have to drag me kicking and screaming. I wasn't complaining. I was glad Jeanie invited us. We have a lot of old friends that we haven't seen in a while and I wanted to see them. Sheree and I have been very close lately (famous last words) and just starting to feel sexual with each other again. We both thought if the time seemed right and we felt right about it and felt up to it, we would perhaps do something together at the party, maybe Sheree would fuck me in the ass with her dildo. Great. But great I wasn't on Saturday. Tired and congested and really bad headache that Percocet wouldn't kill. But I still intended to go. When I'm feeling bad it's a major effort to go out, even when I want to, knowing at the very least I have to be sociable and answer a lot of questions and make small talk. It's all very tiring and in the end, pointless. But the point here is I wanted to go, I wanted to see old friends, and I didn't want to let Sheree down, and maybe—just maybe we'd find the opportunity to feel sexy with each other again, in public, since we were just starting to get the feeling back in private. But fuck, I come home from Debbie's and Sheree's in that bouncing off the walls, mental channel surfing, high and not so mighty altered state. I say it here for the whole world to read (and you, too, Sheree, since you are my world, and I think the world of you), I love Sheree, but *I CAN'T STAND HER WHEN SHE'S STONED*. She drives me nuts. And I have no sexual desire for her whatsoever *WHEN SHE'S STONED!* I underline, cap and put this in bold letters because I want to be understood: I love Sheree more than anything or anyone in the world. I am "the luckiest man on the face of the earth" to have her in my life. I'd be dead without her. But *I CAN'T STAND HER WHEN SHE'S STONED*. I've learned to tolerate it better over the years, but in order to do that I have to distance myself from her, to let her do her thing and have a good time in her altered state, while I try to coexist happily (albeit a bit lonelier) in mine. No such luck. I inevitably get sucked into her angst and her *mishigas*, and it soon becomes a war between the states, a not-so-civil war of words ending in depression and alienation, and here we are. Sex is the big bug-a-boo with this one. It's already a sensitive issue because of age, ill health and the side effects of antidepressants. Add pot to the stew and the fact that the only time she's hot for me is when she's stoned, the time I most want to run from her, it does-n't make for a healthy sex life. The fact that we never seem to get to sex until 2 or 3 in the morning when we're both tired as hell is also not very helpful either. Bad scene at home after the party last night with her trying to finally fuck me in the ass with her big black dildo while I was up doing my drugs, exhausted, terrible headache (not tonight, I have a headache) and still somewhat angry that she got stoned, not once, but twice on a night when we were supposed to be together. Just a few days ago, in the car, Sheree turns to me and says, "I've decided not to get stoned around you anymore. I don't like the way I am around people when I'm stoned. It's something I should do when I'm by myself.

I think you're right about this one," she says. "Uh huh," I say.

7/4/95   Well that's just dandy. Thought I was being so efficient, copying files from the main computer to the Powerbook, but I inadvertently replaced or erased last night's journal entry. I don't even remember what I wrote. It was so late, and I was so tired, there wasn't much writing anyway, but what a stupid thing to do, and I hate the break in continuity. Happy 4th. BOOM! Rita & Kirby and Scott were here. Kirby seemed depressed. Maybe he's sick of me by now. I was sick of everybody. Nervous tonight. I hate party holidays like the 4th of July. I can't wait for everybody to get back to work where they belong. I like work days. Of course I don't have to go to work, so I can afford to like work days. But I like them because they're orderly, and they make sense, and everything and every *one* is in their place. And there is less likelihood of something going wrong. Boy, somebody should take that stick out of my ass.

7/5/95   A respite from the headaches, but heartache nonetheless. Thinking a lot about Tim and why he doesn't call anymore. He talks to Mom a little, but it sounds like he keeps his distance there too. And John—well, I think Mom would like to have her son, John the Baptist's, head on a silver platter all her own. What's with my siblings? I think it's survivor's guilt. They hate me for all the attention I've gotten over the years due to the CF, and they feel guilty for that and for being the healthy ones, the bad ones, the survivors. But fuck it, it's time to grow up. Time is running out. If they want survivor's guilt, I'll give them a whole shit load of survivor's guilt real soon. A lot sooner than they realize. As far as details of the day and the life go: I'm dirty, need a shower and a shave. Finally brushed my teeth. I think they're rotting, but I don't want to do anything about it. Carl was here cleaning up while the painters and roofers were patching up and I was spitting up, as usual. Congested. Bad bad, dizzying headache this morning, but better now, thanks to Mr. P. No real buzz anymore, but it still quells the spells. And speaking of pain,

I again promised Cathy Busby an article on pain for her book. That was last Friday, and still no article. All I am is a pain in the ass with my false promises and procrastination. I took all the 95 journal references to pain and wove them into an 11 page massive tumor. Now I've got to operate on it to see if it's benign or cancerous. And the final detail of the day is I got commissioned by someone at MGM to write ad copy for a film about a guy dying of AIDS who throws himself one last going away party. Am I the right guy for this job or what?

7/6/95 Ugh! Groggy. Upstairs. Fell asleep on the couch while pumping my antibiotics. Infusion confusion. Off track, extra late because we went to the movies with Donna this afternoon. *Belle de Jour*. Best scene: Catherine Deneuvre in bondage, pelted with cow dung. Jack Skelley came over and Sheree barbequed steaks. I wanted no part of barbeque because, like anything else beyond opening a frozen thing for the microwave, it's all too much work for me even to watch. But Sheree was really into it and the food was good. So on the sixth day Bob beheld the barbeque and said, "It is good." What wasn't good was watching old clips of me performing *Wedding of Everything* at Beyond Baroque. So many dumb, embarrassing choices. I actually showed home movies. No irony. No humor. Just those dumb 8mm films of me and the family. What was I thinking? And those songs I was singing. Mr. Improvisation. Mr. Uncool. Ultra geek. What bothers me most about this trash from the past is that if I could make such stupid, creepy, and geeky decisions then, and not know they were stupid, creepy and geeky, then how do I know my aesthetic choices now aren't just as stupid, creepy and geeky? I cringe at the thought of being awful and not knowing it, when everybody else knows it but they won't tell me because they feel sorry for me because, after all, "He's dying… but don't worry, he won't be around much longer to plague us with his stupid, creepy and geeky crap."

7/7/95 Sheree's in the kitchen doing another jigsaw puzzle. I'm at my desk, upstairs, on the big computer, infusing antibiotics, for all the good it does. Felt horrible today. Massive headaches. Extremely short of breath. After a month on the juice I should be much better. Every now and then a little hammer hits my head and I realize: I really am dying. It's not a joke or a performance or a dramatic story. It really could happen at any time. But I'm not done. All these projects: punching bag; confetti casket; icons for the film; pain shots for the film; the video balls installation; videotapes to copy for Shiffler; letters to write; request for the rights to the Steve Allen clip; my book; do I tell people to go fuck themselves who have fucked me over? Saw Dennis Cooper's *Frisk* tonight with Kirby and Rita. Now why did I think of Dennis after I wrote the phrase "Fucked me over?" Could have thought of David Trinidad, Tim or John Flanagan, or any number of people who find it so easy to write me off. But I don't have enough pulmonary function to talk to people any way, so they're doing me a favor. Sheree had to practically drag me out of the house tonight. *Frisk* was fair. The filmmaker didn't really understand the book all that much. He's young. And I'm old. Feeling older all the time.

7/8/95 Infusing on the couch in front of our brand new 32 inch television which Sheree's not sure of yet, not sure it's big enough or bright enough. Save the big box it came in. Might have to take it back. We spent 4 years hating the picture on the last set we bought, threatening to take it back, but never getting around to it, me making excuses for it to assuage Sheree's standard buyer's remorse, but the set really was ugly, ugly on the outside and flat on the inside, no blacks, no contrasts. But I think this one's ok. It seems overly blue to me, but maybe it takes some getting used to. Anyway it's most likely the last tv I'll ever buy. Interesting concept. The last this, the last that. I'm upstairs here typing on the baby Mac because I was showing it off to Ralph Rugoff and his wife, Denise. I showed them how it reads back my writing, the *I'm Only Human* and the *Supermasochistic Bob* pieces. Everyone gets weepy-eyed over *I'm Only Human*. Fortuitous piece of writing there. Health report: lousy. Short of breath to the max. Scale of 1 to 10: 8, when active. Headaches: 7.5, saving 10 for a screamer, which I haven't quite had yet, but I'm waiting. Percocet please.

7/9/95 I'm watching *Per Mason*. Fell asleep while infusing. Groggy all day as a matter of fact. Now I'm watching *Per Mason* with headphones on downstairs. Short of breath setting up the big tv downstairs, plugging in the headphone thing so I can hear the tv and not Sheree's snoring. Ed came over and moved the living room furniture for Sheree, but it looked awful so they moved it back, and Ed lugged the old tv down here, and now I'm watching *Per Mason*. So sue me. Tim called today and things are as good as new in the filial affairs department, but I'm too exhausted to go into detail. Back to *Per Mason*. Back to sleep.

7/10/95 No more drugs. At least no more antibiotics. At least not for awhile. Doesn't mean I'm better, just that I'm as good as I'm going to get on these particular bug busters. But I'm just not feeling so hot. Short of breath with any activity. Exploding brain. Saw Riker today. He patted my shoulder and said he wished he had a miracle for me. My PFT's were lower than they've ever been: 43%. Sinus doctor tomorrow. Riker again next week. In the mean time we've doubled the Prednisone, which should cut the wheezing and boost my energy somewhat, and make me a raving maniac in the process no doubt. Saw Obler today. Talked about the reality of dying. Most of the time it's an abstract thing, something to make art about, something to joke about, something to outwit. But the reality is I won't be here anymore and that makes me want to cry. It makes me nervous. I start thinking of all the projects I want to finish, how much time I've wasted. Obler said I had remarkable courage for hanging in there the way I do, but what's the alternative?

7/11/95 2 am searching all over the place for some kind of tripod attachments to rig up the 35mm camera to take a photo of my face in the throes of orgasm as Sheree rides my dick and chokes me like she used to do in the old days. Aura Rosenberg called us last week from Berlin and wants to include us in her book of orgasmic men. We could use an existing photo, and it doesn't have to be an actual orgasm, it could be pretend, but we all know: I NEVER PRETEND. Besides, we haven't fucked for six months or more, so why not fuck for art? I just need to know I can still do it, and I want a photograph to prove it. Thanks to bumping up the Prednisone I can get the hard-on, but I can't find the fucking hardware to set the camera up correctly. I've been up and down the stairs, all through drawers and cupboards, all over the damn place: again thanks to Prednisone. Went to the sinus doctor today. I'm clogged up up there but don't need surgery. I just need to squirt salt water up my nose and clear the shit out. That's as much fun as drowning.

7/12/95 Again almost 3 am. Again setting up still camera for orgasm shot because we didn't have the right stuff last night. Looks like it's all worked out now. So what about you, Mr. Penis? I'm so irritated all the time from the Prednisone it's hard to think about sex… well, easy to think about it, but it's not so desirable. And the headaches of course don't help. And the pressure of try-ing to get something accomplished, knowing full well that time is of the essence. General nervousness, which helps me breathe, but makes me tense. The good lord giveth and then he fucks you in the ass. Hey! It's *Per Mason* time. I know this is shitty writ-ing. What a legacy. Sometime it's only reporting. The extent of my discipline. A few lousy lines. What we laughingly call a para-graph. What we optimistically call art.

7/13/95 Sleepy on the couch all day. Sleepy while getting pound-ed on at Debbie's. Falling asleep over my Cajun Blackened Steak at Molly's birthday dinner at Figs. Got pissed off and panicky in the Predni-zone trying to make Molly a card on the computer at the last minute when all I really wanted to do was go back to sleep on the couch until I absolutely had to wake up and drag my sorry ass to dinner. Sheree's worried that I'm getting sicker and that's why I keep falling asleep, but that's only partially true. True I'm not feeling all that great, sob, the usual worse than usual congestion and dark, blood streaked phlegm. But I can't sleep at night because of the extra Prednisone I'm taking. That's what I'm doing here now, again 3 am. *Vertigo* on the tv. I fell asleep on the couch. Missed the news. Missed Letterman. Deep sleep. Take some pills. Stumble down here. Boom. Wide awake. But that chasm is narrowing now and I'm none too wide, and it is a wake — the longest wake in the history of man. The Longest Wake. Now there's a film. Zzzzzzzz.

7/14/95 Home, where else. A couple of boring hours at Jon Reise and Jill Goldman's birthday party. Probably not their fault. I roam from room to room, outside, inside, everybody talking but not me. No one I know. Michael and Nancy. No one else. Nice to be invited somewhere, but as soon as I get there I want to leave. "Oh, God, it's only 9:00. We've only been here an hour." Well the cake finally did come and we finally did leave. Just out of sorts. I know it's the Prednisone. Can't find the few Oxazepam I had. Some anti-anxiety pills would be just what the doctor ordered. Yeah, right up my alley. The perfect end to a perfect day. But where the fuck are they? And what the fuck am I watch/not watching on the television? Some depressing Keith Carradine bullshit. And here's the snoring. We're supposed to be fucking, but she's snoring and I'm boring. Snoring and Boring. Thank you Ladies and Germs.

7/15/95 I wuz asleep. But now I'm not. Drugged. Groggy. Headache 8. Sweats. The Prednisone. The Percocet. The Oxazepam. Distracted as I write because I'm watching Jack Nicholson in *Wolf* on tv. Strangely flat and compelling, possibly completely stupid, but queer as hell. Good tv, none the less, for 5 in the morning. As I said, I wuz asleep after returning home exhausted from Dana Duff's birthday party in Culver City. Exhausted from dealing with Sheree, stoned and creative and panicking over her "reading" at some leather lesbian soiree. I got real exasperated, fucking nasty with her. The Prednisone. Spent the whole day in Photoshop putting a birthday cake into a 10 year old photo of Dana and me, and then smack dab in the middle of the cake is my big dick (what else) with a candle in it. I think I'm obsessed with these cyber penises of mine because sex in the real world is so much more difficult these days. We did manage to fuck this morning, if that's what you call it. I tweaked a hard-on for the camera and Sheree stuffed it in and rode it a while as she choked me, and we snapped a few photos, but no coming. The Zoloft. Afterward Sheree did get-off a get off with the assistance of the vibrator on her clit and my teeth on her tit. But later that day it was my fangs in her jugular while trying to help edit her damn lesbian piss tape while she raved and yammered and drove me nuts. I didn't want to be mean. Didn't want to say "Shut up!" But I'm just as out of it on my drugs (Prednisone) as she is on hers (pot). But it all just made me feel shittier and more anxious. More pills, Oxazepam. And Sheree's pretty understanding about the whole thing, or so stoned she doesn't give a shit. So all's right with the world. The sun's coming up. The headache's subsiding (Percocet). And we're watching *Wolf*. The new day awaits. Grrrrrrrr.

7/16/95 The breath grows shorter and shorter. The possibility of the hospital in my immediate future seems likely. Tomorrow. A week before camp. Otherwise camp would be out of the question with this fucked up breathing. But what isn't out of the question? All this ad copy I'm supposed to write for the party movie about death and dying, without dwelling on death or dying. Not that smart. Not that good. And I'm way too tired to try to be tonight.

7/17/95 Very difficult day in the very difficult life. Keep getting these attacks of SOB—shortness of breath. And it *is* a son-of-a-bitch. Extremely thick phlegm. Trying to get things done, to mail a simple package to Mom and Dad, to work at the computer, do some filing, take a fucking shit—it all wipes me out and I'm back on the couch sleeping and watching OJ. How the hell could I go to camp like this? Can't. Going into the hospital tomorrow morning for sure, so maybe I'll feel better by next week. I get this last minute anxiety because I want to tie together all the loose ends of my life around the house here before I get admitted and before I go off to camp. I'll be gone for two weeks. That's two weeks all the work I've procrastinated on these past several weeks will now be put off two more weeks. Time is disappearing right before my eyes. Time is drifting by. Spring flowers are starting to die. I'm looking at Sheree's naked body curled up on the brand new expensive sheets she just bought. She melts into them. She glows blue. The television. *One, Two, Three* with James Cagney. One of her favorite movies but I don't get it yet. Berlin. Ugh!

7/18/95 Here I am back in the hospital. Can barely keep my eyes open. So tired. I want to write a lot and do a lot but I can't keep my eyes open. I already said that. See? It's all reporting. I did did did. I can't can't can't. The news on tv. OJ. The news at home. Worried. Sheree, my parents and me. I am dying, that's old news, but none of us know when it will happen or how long it will take. So each time I get sick, especially within such short time frames, it's natural to wonder if this is it. And what about all the stuff I haven't finished? What are my funeral plans? Sheree, when she's finally convinced that I'm not going to pull out of this one, gets on me about burial or non-burial plans. She wants me to be cremated so she can keep my ashes nearby. My mother would like to have me buried, again close by, close to her. And she'd ultimately like to move my two sisters, Cathy and Tish, from their respective gravesides to one near me, so she could visit all of us together. I'm not sure whether I'm going to do this art piece or not, to bury myself with a video camera and record my decay. If I determine this to be an important piece, then everyone should help me make it a reality. But my mother would never go for it. And Sheree doesn't think it's feasible. And of course Kirby is all gung ho for it because it's the perfect end to the film. But I'm not living for the film. I'm not dying for the film. Well, maybe I'm dying for the film, but I haven't decided on this death piece, nor have I decided how I want it to be when I die. Big party? Casket? Where? But "when?" is the big question. I know it will be soon, but I don't know what soon is either.

7/19/95 Fucking around with Photoshop here on my little computer in my big ol' hospital bed with pains in my chest and phlegm in my lungs and a pounding in my head and a few thoughts like how come Amy never calls me and what kind of an idiot is my fucking brother, John, and how do I want to die, where. Sweaty, leg cramps, congestion. Complaints. Sheree was here again tonight. Sad about me being here. We have this nice home together but we can't share it together because I'm always in here. Don't die, she says. OK. But it's all this crap I have do to stay alive that becomes more and more problematic. Mr. Adjustable. There's a new super hero: Mr. Adjustable. Able to withstand anything because he adjusts to everything. By day he's a whiner and complainer. But by night he's Mr. Adjustable! The news on TV. More shit. More shootings in the workplace. More OJ. More murder. I'd like to write longer and better but my eyes get so tired and my chest hurts. Gotta pee.

7/20/95 My hospital bed office. If I can stay awake. Don't sleep very much at night so I'm groggy most of the day. And doped up on Percocet, but I don't give a fuck because I'm sick of being uncomfortable for this amount of time without getting a hard-on for my trouble. I might be feeling a little bit better tonight. Not as short of breath as previous nights. Amy called earlier and I did my usual bitching. Told her I was pissed off at people like Dennis and David and my Christian brother, John, for abandoning me when I'm dying. I wasn't exactly spreading it on thick in her honor, but I want people to know god dammit that it's true—I'm dying, maybe sooner than later, maybe not, but I'm definitely worse and getting worse. So where are my friends? I told Amy that it bugs me that we only talk when I'm sick. I didn't get pissed off like I should have, but I told her. Peter Huttinger called and I told him I was pretty scared and feeling awful. He always gets quiet when I talk like that. Maybe that's all I'll do is talk like that and rub people's nose in my dying. "Hi, I'm Bob and I'm dying." Meanwhile I've got to get some work done. Have to get this writing better. It's really in a rut now. Have letters to write. My death to attend to. Like how do I want to be buried? Who do I want to please? Myself, Sheree, or Mom and Dad? They got the Steve Allen tape and the *El Pere Et Fils* card. Made them cry. As I said, rub their noses in it. I'm so cute. The cutest dying person.

7/21/95 I don't know what to write in here anymore. The same old story every night. Headache blah blah blah hospital blah blah blah can't breathe blah blah blah dying blah blah blah tv blah blah blah Sheree blah blah blah Mom and Dad blah Tim blah stupid brother John blah blah letters to write blah blah blah camp blah my penis blah blah list keeping and blah blahs a poor substitute for real writing blah blah blah blah blah not enough pain killers blah blah but if the breathing's bad enough on Monday Riker might up the pain meds because what have we got to lose blah blah blah blood in my phlegm blah blah blah vital signs not so blah blah vital no change no up no down blah blah lost in the blah blah and the pain med but the pain's still here and there's no rush anymore blah blah blah whah whah whah why won't this nurse clean out my phlegm basin huh blah huh this is so awful I don't deserve to live blah.

7/22/95 A room change. The floor was flooded in the other room, so here I am in this one, high and dry. Dry anyway. Percocet barely quells the head pounding. Nothing to get high about. Speaking of high, Sheree isn't. Once again very depressed. Once again not taking Paxil, not since Tuesday. Once again a morning after evening of wine and pot, throwing up and feeling out of it. I think most of it's the Paxil. I knew she stopped it when I talked to her yesterday. And she wasn't depressed yesterday. But I could hear it in her voice. And lo and behold she's low today. She's out tonight, not answering the phone. So here I am alone in my bed, nobody to talk to, tired again, writing crap, nothing on tv, eyes too tired to read, bored with these dumb computer games, not creative enough to do any meaningful work on the damn thing, putting off my letters and my articles and my ad copy and my fax replies, nodding off, no snack tonight cause those fuckers forgot it or someone stole it goddamn it, but I'm too tired to eat any hoo. I'll sleep for a bit and then I'll come back.

7/23/95 So why not try writing in the daylight hours, before I'm dead to the world? The question is, when am I *not* dead to the world? When I'm talking to Mom. She just called. Not that I put on an act when I'm talking to her, but she always thinks I'm more depressed than I actually am in the first place, so I do try to temper my feelings when she calls. Like now, I didn't let on how down Sheree was on the phone a few minutes ago, and how pissed I got about it, and how it does depress me to listen to her continue to go on about how out of the loop WE are, how nobody wants OUR work how WE could drop off the face of the earth and nobody would give a shit about US. The point is she doesn't give a shit about herself and she's constantly wanting the rest of the world to make up for the deficit. Paxil fills the gap. Like patching the holes in her head with spackle. But if she stops spackling, there's the holes. And there I am, blowing air through the cavities, trying to get her to listen to me. Cut it out. Stop wasting my time. Stop wasting OUR time. Yeah, I get pissed off too. I knew about this video show that includes everyone in the world but us. We were sitting on the couch together reading our mail when I got the postcard and its list of aesthetic in crowd which we were out of. Yes it pissed me off, but I stashed the card so Sheree wouldn't see it and then I went on with what's left of my miserable life.

Back in bed. Back "home." Faux home. Home away from home, the hospital, after a brief pass so I could make it to the first night of the CF campfire. Sheree picked me up. Her mood a bit better, thanks to my stern lecture no doubt. The camp was difficult and strange. Always strange to come into it rather than start off as a part of it. But it was hard for me because it was so hard to breathe. Talk about your fish out of water. That's me. A big blowfish, huffing and puffing. Somebody should flush me down the toilet. The camp itself struck me as sad and pathetic. A shadow of its former self. Only 40 kids, as opposed to the usual 80 or more. Old and tired counselors. I kept staring at this fat bald guy, wondering who he was—turns out to be Steve Henkle! And the people who aren't there make it sad. No Ivan Harwood and his bass. No Paige and her body. No sex appeal. Not many kids. No energy or air (on my part). But we carry on. Banging and squawking out the tried and true songs for the tried and true blue. I tried to be funny, calling everybody pathetic, trying to pump myself full of energy by being the fake mean guy, but calling everybody pathetic was hitting too close to home because that *was* my first impression. But all's right with the world here in my freshly made bed, my roast beef sandwich snack, and my Percocet and other pharmaceuticals. We'll try the campfire cameo again tomorrow and see what happens the rest of the week. Tomorrow morning more PFT's and blood gasses to see how I'm progressing, or how I'm not.

7/24/95 The old fashioned way: writing by hand because, unfortunately, the computer is still in Sheree's trunk and is long gone. She and Kirby came down and she sprung me for another camp visit. Drive from the hospital directly to the campfire, already in progress, try to catch up with the flow, diminished though it is, huff and puff *Down in the Easy Chair*, make a few jokes, lead but don't get too involved in "The Blue Jay Song" because 'The Blue Jay Song will kill me. All in all, my brief appearance was extremely difficult. Feel so peaceful and calm now — but anxious and short of breath, bloated head, bulging eyes, coughing, slobbering, gasping old codger, a shadow of my former self, a relic, but I go on — boy do I go on. I won't go back until Wednesday, and then I'll stay until it's over — the camp that is.

7/25/95 Late late late. I'm infused by the nurse. Nebulized by a big armed ex-Marine. All this for little ol' me. Pump me up. Going home tomorrow (today). Home just long enough to get my stuff and go to camp. Too tired to write. I'll be home soon. Get back to my routine. Don't really want to go to camp — cause I don't really want to go anywhere. It's all a constant effort. Just want to be alone.

7/26/95 Back home. Back in bed. Back with Sheree. Back to the computer. Supposed to be at camp. Tonight was the costume party and dance. The plan was to check out of the hospital, come home, pick up my antibiotics, pack up and head down there. But once home I couldn't bear leaving again. Just getting dressed in the hospital was an effort. It's so comfortable and peaceful here at home, I can't stand the thought of leaving again. And there's so little for me to do there now. I stopped fitting in at camp years ago. Now that my participation is cut down even more by the crappy way I feel most of the time it's harder and harder for me to drag my ass down there. We were going to get up at 5:00 am tomorrow and make it to camp in time for the wake up songs in the cabins. But then I started thinking, what? Maybe I'm getting old, but nothing seems worth it anymore. The more energy it takes to do things the more it just doesn't seem worth it. So I'm here in bed, ear plugs, headphones, television. Feeling depressed, have to admit. Discombobulated. Yanked from one setting to another. Pumped up, but the base line never seems to improve enough for me to feel it for very long. There is an improvement from last week it's just that it nothing to write home about, or write in this computer about… anymore tonight.

7/27/95 "We thought we could sit forever in fun, but our chances really were a million to one." Couldn't bring myself to get to camp any earlier than 6 pm tonight, just in time for the Cajun cook out and time enough for me to sit around the campfire and play the guitar and sing the old ditties, as well as a couple of improvs and *Supermasochistic Bob* to boot. Considering I lay around here all day wondering how it was I was going to do any-thing ever again, it's a miracle I dragged my ass down there with Sheree and Kirby and slipped into the groove, singing the songs like I'd never been gone. It helped my psyche immensely when I realized I didn't have to sleep over tonight and I didn't have to spend the whole day there tomorrow in the blazing heat. I'm too much the homebody now. Except for the hospital, I can't stand being away from home for any period of time. Besides, there's nothing I'm able to do at camp except sing a few songs, so tonight's plan worked out perfectly. Tomorrow we'll drive down in time for the last dinner and the last campfire, some more singing, some hugging, some crying, some sad goodbye's, and then back here to this comfy bed with its expensive finely woven sheets and the television, and the Pee Boy and his new piss foun-tain, and my computer, and my life, for as long as I have it. I'm amazed I had any reserve left at all. Suddenly I could not only breathe, but I could shape that breathing into some decent singing, not like it used to be, but what I now lack in physical ability I make up for with experience and a sense of showman-ship that I've picked up along the way. If I wanted to I could real-ly do something with the singing, even now, even with the oxy-gen. I'd be unique, that's for sure. Who wouldn't give the pathet-ic oxygen boy a chance?

7/28/95 What a relief. Home from the last night of camp, the last campfire, the last roundup for me, and somehow I pulled it off. I sang at the campfire. I went around to the cabins and sang good-night songs, I sang dirty improvs at the counselor meeting, I passed out New Museum posters for the counselors, and through it all I sang well, I was funny, and I could breathe. Somehow when it's time I get this reserve of energy and stamina that amazes me. But I planned it this way. I only went to camp at night when it was cool. I'm still on antibiotics. I slept during the day. I paced myself. And now I'm home. And now I'm done. I was still a part of camp without having to be at camp, in the heat, in the dust, with the bugs and the boredom and the work.

Not that it wasn't work for me, it was, starting with the hellish drive. And it took every ounce of oxygen to get those songs out, but I did it and I did it well. I even broke in the "Super masochistic Bob" song and they loved it, both the clean version and the real version. I feel kind of weird about the last *Jenny* improv and the *Suck My Jesus* song. A little over the top perhaps, but that's what they asked for. After a long week of hard work, and the sadness of the last campfire where the kids remember all their dead friends, I perform kind of a service by singing these ridiculous over the top songs. I relieve the tension of the week. I'm as close as they get to getting drunk. But I still feel kind of weird about it. But fuck it, I'm home. Obligations done. Naked now. TV. My own work. Fucking Sheree. Kirby's film. My life and what's left of it.

7/29/95 July is slipping away. Late night here in bed. Humid tonight. Both of us naked on top of the blankets, well, I still have my underwear on because Donna's spending the night so proper guest etiquette demand I keep some clothes on anyway. Now Sheree's under the covers, but not me. Donna's in Sheree's office. We saw the movie *Kids* this afternoon. Teenagers fucking. Like no kids I ever knew. I didn't fuck until I was 17, maybe 18. Becky, at the Fairfax Motel, with *They Drive by Night* on the television, and a little kitchenette where we cooked Spaghettios. It was the first time for both of us and it was barely a fuck at all. She was very tight and in tremendous pain, so I kept pulling back, going very slowly. Finally I just used my fingers, first one finger, then two, etc. I don't know if I actually fucked with my dick all the way inside her that night or not. We fucked for a couple of years after that, but that's all I remember about the first night. Just a minute: Sheree's snoring: ear plugs in. Underwear off. There's the famous dick. Where's Becky? No one seems to know. So now that I'm home from camp and home from the hospital, what is it I need to do with myself? 1. Finish the article for Cathy Busby, since I was too much of a spineless wimp to say no, I don't want to be part of your dumb book. 2. Mail Steve

Allen tape and some my recent Photoshop collages to Tim, along with a letter or note telling him I'm glad we can still talk blah blah blah just so things stay patched up with us and I maintain my status as a good guy. 3. Call my other brother, John the Baptist, and tell him to go soak his head. 4. Ship *Superman* print to New Museum. 5. Copy tapes for Shiffler. 6. Ship stuff for Peter. 7. Call the punching bag guy in New York. 8. Scan more photos. 9. Make mock coffin with model of me in it for video "infomercial" about *The Viewing*. 10. Illustrate *Mop and Broom* for Kirby. 11. Scan more icons Kirby. That's enough. What I'll probably do instead of any of this is watch OJ all day and sleep on the couch, come to bed, write crap like this, and take a Percocet or two with a Vicodin thrown in for that extra effervesce, and try to get into a deep enough sleep that I might even dream something.

7/30/95 Tired again. Late again. Full of barbequed turkey dogs and beans. Late dinner cause I had to go to Debbie's. I went to the market and Sheree bar-b-queued and we both ate and watched archeological nature shows. Suddenly I sense Sheree a bit distant. She mumbles something about us being as mismatched as Donna and Jeffrey. What? Now she's questioning herself, I can tell. Wondering what the fuck she's doing with the likes of me. This on the heels of missing me and wanting me back home no matter what condition I was in. Well I'm here, and I'm in comparatively good condition, even Debbie was impressed, but I sense Sheree's having her doubts again. And now she's snoring too. Dreaming of a better life without me perhaps. In spite of the sadness and loss surrounding our present situation, I still feel I gave her everything she asked for: a great sex life, a great art collaborator, a partner who was a star of sorts, a partner who was imaginative, creative, and absolutely devoted to her. But whatever she gets, there's always something else she doesn't get. And no matter how much she praises me and dotes on me one day, it's always followed by the other foot, the "what the fuck?" foot, the foot that she kicks herself in the ass with as she says to herself "I have wasted my life."

Of course this is all conjecture on my part, based on insecurities built on past experience. I could be wrong. It's been known to happen.

7/31/95 Tony Perkins and Burl Ives on tv. Two dead guys. Tony Perkins, Burl Ives, and me. Two dead guys and one on the way. Talked about camp, death and dying with Obler today. He was concerned about those final moments, when I'm no longer breathing on my own. Would I still be conscious? Would I feel as though I was strangling when they took me off the respirator? But I won't be on a respirator. Thing is I don't know what the final minutes are like. I could just have a heart attack and let it go at that. My ankles have been swelling up lately. Heart could be working overtime. Gotta buckle down and get my work done. Pain article due. What a pain. How do I get into these things? Why is my neighbor driving my car and getting it smashed up when I don't drive it but keep shelling out money to keep it running? I'm the consummate nice guy. I rationalize it by reasoning that Alex does a lot of work around here, and he's a nice guy too, so it's the least I could do. It's probably my way for atoning for the humiliating fact that we always have to turn to Alex for a lot of the simple repair jobs and emergencies that I used to be able to deal with but couldn't possibly handle now. So my penance is giving up my wheels. It's just too bad Alex is not as capable as I was. In 15 years I never had a single accident. In a few weeks he's already gotten the fender smashed by some guy in a pickup truck with no insurance and a phony phone number. Time to sell the damn thing. I don't drive it anymore anyway.

8/1/95 New month, same old body, feeling older than it is or will ever have the chance to be. I'm afraid my heart's starting to give out. My ankles have been swelling up since last week when I was Mr. Troubadour at camp. In contrast to the great burst of energy I had "way" back then, today I can barely move without being severely short of breath, and can barely stay awake when I'm not moving. While trying to help Sheree with the Pee Boy fountain this morning I couldn't help stepping outside myself to catch the irony of me huffing and puffing trying to get our naked white nasty dick-holding boy to pee in the bowl properly, working up a sweat trying to get the pump connected the right way, frustrated as hell cause my own pump felt so fucked, my connections all kinked and haywire, and even my dick not much good or much use to anyone. Feeling sorry for myself I guess. But if not me, then who? What bothers me most is that it's so hard to do work. I just want to lay around all day and watch tv. I have 20 or 30 different projects or commitments to work on, not to mention the IV antibiotics, the breathing treatments, Debbie, pharmacies, doctor's appointments — how can I resist just curling up on the couch, watching OJ, and saying, "Fuck it?"

8/2/95 Sheree has these doo-hickies hanging on the bed posts that are driving me crazy. They're necklaces and everytime I move they clang against the metal posts and, irritable fuck that I am, it drives me nuts. But I've been real irritable and pissed about everything today because I'm sick and tired of being sick and tired. I can't do anything anymore. Been dozing on the couch all day. Couldn't help Sheree put up the curain rods in the bedroom. Scott had to, and that embarrasses me. I'm a long way from the slave I was. Right now Sheree's squeezing my dick and banging it against my foot. That feels good. As long as I don't have to move. Going to see Riker tomorrow to see what's going on with this fluid thing. All I know is my ankles are squishy and my chest feels like it's got a rock in it and I'm real short of breath whenever I try to do anything. That's it for now, my bevy of compaints. Afraid I'm going to die. Afraid I won't get my projects done. Wondering where the energy's going to come from to even stay awake when I want to. The only thing I have kept up on is this journal. I've only missed two or three days since December. Yeah, but what's he writing like? Shit mostly, but who's... who's... *dozing*...dozing?.. sleeping. Me. Up at dawn for more drugs.

8/3/95 Flat on my back in bed cause the infusion pump keeps beeping when I sit up, probably due to the fucked up porta-cath. I'm exhausted as hell, can't keep my eyes open. Tired all the time, when I'm not totally incopacitated or out of breath, probably due to the fact that I'm dying, what else? Saw Riker today. $PCO2$ is 66. Not good. That, and the fact that it's 2 am, is why I keep dozing. There's more to write, but I'm just too tired.

8/4/95 Still tired. Still infusing. Still late. So tired I didn't even leave the house to go to Debbie's. Slept on the couch instead. Work day. More video interview with Kirby all day. Saw the camp footage, me singing around the campfire and inside the cabins. I'm amazed at how good I sounded and how much energy I had just a few days ago. Now I'm a wreck. But I'm going to sing again on Sunday at the Bob Flanagain Pre-Memorial Weenie Roast at Beyond Baroque. The title was my idea. They wanted to use me as a draw for their weenie roast fund raiser. I said fine, but call it "The Bob Flanagan Pre-Memorial Weenie Roast." Since I did so well at camp Sheree's encouraging me to sing camp songs at the weenie roast. I will, but only songs that have to do with death and departure. *Knockin' on Heaven's Door, I Shall be Released, In My Tomb, Fun to be Dead,* I'm dwelling on the death stuff because more and more I feel I'm getting close to it. Death itself doesn't bug me. I'm sure it will eventually, but right now it's still too abstract. But what's really bugging me is I know I'm going to be laid up, in the hospital and out of the hospital, taken away from home, away from Sheree, away from the computer, away from work. Even if I don't go into the hospital as much, as Sheree would prefer, that's not the issue. It's how sick I am and how incapacitated I am. The confetti coffin is a great idea. I can see it in people's eye when they hear about it or when they see the sheet of photos I've scanned so far. But that's just the tip of the iceberg. There are hundreds and hundreds of photos left to scan. And then there's the legwork necessary to get the damn thing done. How can I do that AND sleep on the couch all day? I know I'm running out of time. I haven't scanned anything in months. I was fooling myself thinking these journal notes were shaping up into some kind of usable writing, but it's just diary shit. Of interest to me and me alone. Not even good writing. Again I have this stupid obligation to put together this "pain" article for Cathy Busby. How many times did I say no to this? How come I'm still laboring over it? I thought I would just compile all of the references to pain and pharmaceuticals that have appeared in the journal so far, the same thing I did with *Cough.* It marginally worked for *Cough,* but the truth is it sucks here. So now I'm trying to make some sense out of it to come up with five pages of something even though I'm not getting paid anything for this, and even though I don't recognize any of the other writers in the anthology, and even though I hate the title of the anthology, *When Pain Strikes,* and even though I barely know Cathy Busby and I don't owe her anything, and even though Dr. Obler would think I was an idiot for doing it, and even though the deadline was last Monday — fuck it, I'm still doing it. *The Pain Journal.* I thought it would make me write something great. But when you don't have it in you, you don't have it in you. I need to be able to write great things again and write them fast because eventually, probably sooner than later, that's all I'm going to have left is the writing and it damn well better be good.

8/5/95   Late drugs because we were over at Rita and Kirby's watching a recent cut of the *Bobumentary*. There are good segments, but more segments are needed and then there needs to be a way to weave all the segments together. Sometimes the more I watch it or get involved with it, the less interesting I become. I took three Percocets tonight and I feel pretty good, but I'm tired, real tired, always tired. Tomorrow death songs at Beyond Baroque, "The Bob Flanagan Pre-Memorial Weenie Roast." In the meantime, tonight, I've had it. I'm done. Turn me over.

8/6/95   No wonder the writing here is so atrocious. I only write at the end of the day when I'm the most exhausted and all I want to do is go to sleep, watch tv or jack off (well "jack" anyway, I hardly ever get "off" these days). Watching Hitchcock's wierd depressing film, *The Wrong Man* with Henry Fonda. Depressing film at the end of a good day. Starting off with a nice slow fuck with Sheree this morning. No coming on either of our parts. Too old, too sick, too Paxiled up and Zolofted out. But it was nice to be inside her. And later this afternoon was the *Bob Flanagan Pre-Memorial Weenie Roast*. I sang *Down in the Easy Chair, In My Tomb, Knockin' on Heaven's Door, Night Rider's Lament, I Shall Be Realeased, Brand New Teneseee Waltz, Supermasochisiticbob*, and *Fun to be Dead* with Jack Skelley. Good response. I hardly seemed sick at all. Now I'm wiped out. Can't type any more.

8/7/95   Laptop getting a modem implant so I can be on line all the time. It's hard to write with *Emmanuelle in Bankok* on the tv — but I'll try. Anyway, with the modem at least I'll have the option to be online. What little "onlining" I've done seems dull and boring to me so far. And when you get into the depths of shit like "abusive chat rooms" or "chat rooms for the abused," the way Ed seems to be obsessed these days, it's downright depressing. Mainly a modem is a cheap way to communicate when I'm in the hospital. Slight — very slight — chance I may be back there yet again, the hospital, if this pressure in my chest turns out to be pericarditis. I tend to doubt it now. The pain was intense over the weekend, and even earlier this evening when I went to Debbie's, but right now it feels fine. Echocardiogram tomorrow will reveal me as the alarmist idiot I truly am. Speaking of heartattacks, let's get back to *Emmanuelle*.

8/9/95 Sheree was going to pick up the laptop today but she forgot, so I'm on manual. Feeling anxious and annoyed the past couple of days. Forgot to take my Prednisone one day. That may account for it. Still feel horribly bloated, even though there's no sign of fluid around my heart, if I can believe the skills of the technician who ran my test. I'm 145 pounds and I know that's not fat or muscle. It makes me feel sluggish and short of preath, but forget the complaining. Cleaned up some of the Pain Journal and faxed it to Cathy Busby. No response. She's probably pissed. I have tons of work to do for her, Kirby, Peter — and lil' ol' me.

8/10/95 Laptop's back. Modemized. Can't wait to go into the hospital again so I can go in and be connected at the same time. Just signed on and talked to Ed in his "abuse survivors" chat room. It's like walking into a party full of weird people I don't want to talk to but had to go because I knew Ed would be there and I wanted to say hi. Well I said hi. Then I said bye. I've got tons of shit to do. Now the main computer's fucked. Started making weird noises, so I shut it down and then the external hard drive disappeared. Nothing's backed up either. Fucked. Maybe. Hope not. Now that I'm up, it's down. And I've got so much to do: the torture machine drawings for Kirby. The bed of nails and coffin info for Peter. And don't forget that grand pain in the ass: *When Pain Strikes*. In the meantime I managed to carve an apple head and put it into a box with the infra-red video camera attached. The test run for the "infomercial" test run of *The Viewing*. It looks damn good. Been really anxious today. Probably due to all I have to do. God am I dirty. And I need a shave. I did manage to brush my teeth. Isn't that great? I'm so proud of myself. In the mean time I'm filling up with fluid. I feel like a water baloon or the Stay Puff Marshmallow Man. How sweet it ain't.

8/11/95 Ants are crawling in and out of my teeth and around my eye sockets and my nostrils. The moisture is draining out of me and I'm starting to shrivel up. My little apple head effigy looks great. And today I also did a pretty good drawing for the Bobumentary: it's a drawing/ montage of "me" with a big hard on, standing at a dark room enlarger to which I've attatched a needle, something I did 20 years ago because I couldn't get up the nerve to stick a needle in my dick without automating it this way. Now, at Kirby's request, I'm in the process of illustrating this and other auto-erotic "torture" machines I've designed over the years. And they're working out real well, despite the fact that the computer kept giving hell. Sheree had to take the external drive in for repairs. It's ok, and so is my stuff. Not only is the computer fucking up (Photoshop was also a real stubborn bitch today, too) but my body is still on the fritz, even though I'm feeling better and doing more. I'm all filled up with fluids, from my right armpit, to my ankles, with a large protruding abdoman in between. Looks like I'm pregnant. Feels like I've had an enema. More to worry about. But now I've got to sleep.

8/12/95 I feel like Superman, Underdog, Popeye — not the macho heros, the bloated Thanksgiving day balloons. I feel like I'm walking on the moon. One small step for man, one giant leap closer to the grave. I'm the Pillsbury Doughboy, overdone, crumbling. *Nothin says lovin like somethin in a coffin. Heh, heh!* I'm really feeling the pressure of having to get my life in order before my body gives out entirely. The dying part will be easy (for me), but the constant interruptions, the drives down to the doctor's in Long Beach (even Kirby's had it with that), the drug deliveries that don't come, the oxygen which runs out in the middle of a movie, assuming I have enough energy to drag my ass out of the house to go to a movie, the true humiliation of having to watch Sheree work like a dog to take care of me who used to get so hot being her slave, sickness or no sickness, what a whining wimp I've become, "no" is the first word out of my mouth, it's part of my breathing now, *no… no… no…* I see it like a knife in Sheree's back everytime she hears it, and she's getting tired of it, too, but I'm doing the best I can, that's my mantra these days, but so what?, it doesn't take the sadness away, and maybe I'm not always doing the best I can. I ain't no superhero, that's for sure, and this is no fucking holiday.

8/13/95 Sheree wants to tie me up in our little garden, our little backyard, but not tonight. Still too bloated. Had moments of feeling really terrible today, like I was going to have a heart attack or somethig. Had a big breakfast at Rae's with Molly and Sheree, but not much other food. Again, the bloat. Checking it out tomorow, if necessary. Last night was filled with dreams of the bloat and visions of death, people telling me I'm dying. I'm not dying now, this instant, but I'm dozing, so I'd better knock it off and sleep it off.

8/14/95 Don't tell anybody, but it's really 5 am on the 15th. I fell asleep on the couch while watching Letterman and woke up not knowing where I was, but here I am downstairs in bed pretending I didn't miss a day of writing. Well, it's still dark outside, so I'm still calling it the night of the 14th. The night John finally calls after a year or more of being incomunicado. Just as I suspected, despite Mom's and Sheree's supositions that his silence had something to do with his religious convictions, that had nothing to do with it. He basically has no balls, plus he's kind of dumb and takes whatever people say to him literally. So if Mom in the heat of anger says, "I never want to speak to you again," John obliges by not calling for two years. So why not call me? Fear that I'd pull the big brother routine. He's frozen in time, still a kid with Mom, afraid of her wrath; still my little brother, bowing to my tyranny. But fuck all that, he's also lazy and procrastinating and dug himself into a hole, painted himself into a corner, and half a dozen other choice cliches I won't enumerate because this is getting too long and boring already. The upshot is I had a feeling he was going to call soon if I didn't call him first. I set the wheels in motion at camp a few weeks ago when I ragged on John to Bob Cook, knowing full well it would get back to him and he would eventually call. Well it did and he did. I wasn't so much the big brother tonight as I was the wise old soul who's seen it all and knows what's in everyone's heart, blah blah blah. "Forget about the past," I say, "and focus on the future. We're all headed for a difficult time, and if you can convince Mom that you'll be there for her, and for me, things will be better." Bob Cook probably gave John a report how awful I've been feeling because the one thing he did say that was accurate, and was main reason I was going to call him, is that he didn't want my funeral to be the next time he sees or talks to Mom and Dad. "Don't worry," I said. "If you hadn't of called, Mom wouldn't have let you come to the funeral." Mom's another story. She's been hurt, sure, but she set herself up for some of it. And when she's hurt, she's a hard nut to crack, plays a lot of mind games, and also paints herself into a corner. But that's another story. The sun is rising; my alter ego, the Pee Boy, is glistening in the morning dew, but he's not pissing because, like me, his plumbing is all fucked up. A new day is dawning, fraught with possibilities. Fraught with fraught is more like it.

8/15/95 Bob Flanagan, artist, masochist and one of the longest living sufferers of cystic fibrosis, lost his battle this week with the killer disease, a genetic disorder of the lungs and pancreas, that both plagued and empowered the provocotive performer throughout his difficult but productive life.

Born in New York City on December 26, 1952, Flanagan was in and out of hospitals most of his life. Doctors gave him little chance of survival past the age of six or seven years, but survive he did, well beyond anyone's expectations. The difficulties of being sick became the backbone of his work and his masochism.

As a teenager in Orange County, California, Flanagan was the poster boy for the local chapter of the Cystic Fibrosis

Foundation, only to turn the foundation on its ear years later when he became, as he often called himself, "the poster boy from hell" with the 1993 Re/Search publication, *Bob Flanagan Supermasochist.*

At his bedside was his long-time partner, artistic collaborator and dominatrix, Sheree Rose, who was the impetus for Flanagan's most interesting and controversial works, including the infamous *Fuck Journal* in 1986, and the video and performance piece *Bob Flanagan's Sick,* in 1989, which earned Flanagan dubious fame as "the guy who nailed his dick to a board."

Flanagan is survived by his two brothers, Timothy and John; and his parents Robert and Catherine who previously lost two other children to cystic fibrosis, Catherine, at 6 months, and Patricia, who was 21 years of age.

8/16/95 Yesterday's writing all went into the obituary that Kirby wanted for the Bobumentary. Today, most of the day, we recorded new bits for the film: Needles in the baby; reading an old slave contract. Also tried to do Premiere video editing but I just don't know it well enough — somebody's screaming outside at 3 in the morning. Hmmmm. Howling. A dog? A person acting like a dog? Coyote? Sheree says open the door. "No, are you crazy?" Here comes a police helicoptor. There goes a police helicoptor. It's an animal in distress. Maybe another famous black football hero has murdered his blonde ex-wife.

8/17/95 I feel a tiny bit depressed or out of sorts tonight, three days after decreasing my Zoloft to 20mg instead of 40 in the hopes of regaining some of my orgasmic capabilities. Hard-ons do seem to be more frequent, and I almost feel I'm on the verge of coming, but it still comes down to being too much work. And speaking of work, I feel more distracted and out of focus. Didn't get anything accomplished. Of course it doesn't help that Sheree had me up watching some dumb movie with Drew Barrymore till all hours of the morning. Whatever the reason I notice a slight down shift in my mood, increased feelings of lonliness and anxiety over my work and my friends (or imagined lack of), the same irritating, angst filled thoughts I've had before, but where it used to feel like a cut or a scratch, now it's a cut or a scratch that itches like it's geting infected. Maybe that extra 20mg of Zoloft is like an ointment on my psychological cuts, of which these days there are, needless to say, many.

8/18/95 Fought with Ms. S. tonight, or read her the riot act, or vented steam in my Zoloft reduced induced sensitiviy and exasperation with her stoned shrieking and craziness. After dinner at Figs with Molly, Murray, Richard and Ted, I drove her to a birthday party at Robin P.'s, but she lived in some sprawling apartment complex in the hills of Silverlake, all the way in the back, all the way up. Sheree's out of the car looking for the apartment while I wait for her to tell me what she's going to do. She disappears out of sight around the side of the building. Should I leave or what? There she is, yelling for me to come over. Then she starts screaming at me that I'm not helping her, even though I'm right there waiting, not complaining, waiting, driving, figuring where the hell Robin lives because it wasn't where Sheree said it was, but … fuck it. Now she's sleeping and I'm falling asleep. I just wanted her to get the idea that she shouldn't automatcally start yelling at me and hassling me every time she gets stoned. She got it. And we're still lovey dovey. If I just wasn't so tired. (At 3am?). See if I produce something besides phlegm tomorrow.

8/19/95 Sue drove Sheree home from the lesbian "Flog-a-thon." Lots of sucking and cooing and blubbering on the couch next to Sheree. I never used to mind these overt sexual cominglings with other people right in front of my face. In fact it used to turn me on, whether or not the comingler was male or female. Since I was Sheree's slave there was nothing I could do about it, and the humiliation of course was arousing — most of the time. But now I'm an old fogey and I just wanted Sue, as much as I like her, I wanted her to get her face out of Sheree's armpit or crotch or whereever the hell she had it and get it the hell home so we could be alone. It's not that I don't like her company. *Wages of Fear* was on tv, and it was fun watching that together whenever Sue came up for air. What? Am I jealous? Yes, I guess I am. I don't want anyone to take Sheree away from me yet. I have so little to offer her sexually compared to these hot SM lesbians or god forbid if she let a guy near her. So I am more sensitive in that area than I had reason to be in the past. It's hard to be passionate and unbridled and hot to trot when you're short of breath just getting off the couch to take a piss. And the Zoloff drains whatever's left in the desire department. Cutting down on that seems to have pumped me up a little. Hard-on this morning, almost of the verge of coming but I got tired and gave up the ghost and went upstairs to have bagels and cream cheese with Sheree. Oy gevalt!

8/20/95 My dick's in the way. My dick's too big for me to write. It's in my way. It makes my laptop off balance. Starting to get a little hard while I try to write. Write what? Sarah's coming tomorrow. What do we do when she gets here and will it involve my dick? No, of course not. She's just coming to visit her hero, and heroes have to be careful. Careful of what? Too tired to say much. Tom Dennison's last night in L.A. He came over and we showed him Kirby's latest cut of the film. He liked it. It's good. But I'm out.

8/21/95 Up late waiting for our kid for the week, Sarah, to come home. Sheree's fault, turning her over to Andy. Here she is all cozy and safe watching *The Human Animal* on The Learning Channel with old fogies Bob and Sheree till Sheree calls Andy and "poof" like *I Dream of Andy* he appears with yet another new bondage babe-ette on his arm who wants to meet the famous Bob and Sheree, but Sheree's starting to sound an awful lot like Mae, Sarah's Mom, telling Andy everything Sarah's into and not into and what she wants to see and do and I'm thinking Sheree should shut up, maybe Sarah is too shy to say it but maybe she doesn't want to go out clubbing with 'I Dream of Andy," but "SHAZAM" all of a sudden Sarah shows up with black lipstick and a skimpy little t-shirt with the word "POW" emblazond across her suddenly ample breasts and there they all are, out the door to God knows where, and here we are, the famous Bob and Sheree, naked in bed playing computer Solitaire and watching tv, and wondering if we'll ever see our young Sarah again, God knows we'll never see the old Bob and Sheree again — but wait, in between Solitaire hands Sheree squeezes balls and pinches my dick and I get hard and it feels good and I feel like I have a pretty good threshold again and the little bit of pain that's there still feels good — hey, there's a glimmer of the old Bob — this is job for "SUPERMASOCHIST!" He's not dead yet. He's still there somewhere, now that the evil effects of the wonderous yet libido sapping Zoloft have worn off. But forget all that, it's 4 in the morning. Do we know where our cystic is? No.

8/22/95 Now I'm up waiting for Sheree AND Sarah. Not really waiting, just up, barely. Searching the rooms in AOL. Boring. Hot for something sexy, sometimes. Comes in waves, except I just can't come. Hard-ons a plenty, but no climax. Is that Sheree I hear, or Sarah? This will not be one of the sad or exciting pieces of writing. This is just fulfilling my comittment to myself to write something everyday. Today's news is the doctor: echocardiagram: no fluid or enlargement there; stomach x-ray: no fluid or organs out of whack there; so what's causing this crap I feel? Cystic fibrosis, stupid. And the clot around my porta cath, that's going to have to be removed and stuck somewhere else because that's where the real kink is that's screwing up the works, my works, my veins like a bent up garden hose. Speaking of garden hose, say bye to Mr. Penis, asleep as usual, dreaming of Sheree, who's off with the dykes in pussyland.

8/23/95 Up too damn late for no damn reason. Sarah's out again, but that's not it; she's not the reason, not directly. It's Sheree. Sheree, but I'm too tired to go into it. She's stoned. That's all ya need to know. Haranguing me and once again talking shit, this time don't I want Sarah to tie me up? Nope. Why not? dsss...

hours later, after falling asleep, after leaving Sheree upstairsd-
dddddddddddddddddddddddddddddddddddddddddddddd... still
falling asleep, my fingers ddddddddddddddddddddddddddddddd
dddddddddddddddddddddddddddddddddddddddddddddddddffffffff...
again, with the headphones on, the tv on, Sheree out cold next
to me, the sun up and coming, the Pee-boy glistening, again I'm
ddddddddddddddddhhhhhhhhhhhhhhjdddddddddd... sleeping. I got
pissed at Sheree and stormed upstairsfhhhhhv... after getting fed
up with her inebriated insistence that I should feel something
sexual or lustful toward Sarah because she's a beautiful 18 year
old woman with cystic fibrosis who happens to be in love with
me (says Sheree) and I should do who knows what with her, but
I don't know what Sheree has in mind cause Sheree's out of her
fucking mind and no amount of explaining or insistence that she
shut up and mind her own beeswax will ddddddddddddddd
dddddddd (sleep again, slug digits)... I like Sarah. But she's 18
and I'm 42. That wouldn't matter if there were some sort of sexual spark there, but there isn't (and why in hell would Sheree
want there to be one there?). I feel more like a baby-sitter than
a role model. The point is I do hold back because at this point
in my life I don't need a new emotional entanglement. If Sarah
does have some hot fantasies about me, let her go home with
them intact. She doesn't need to be fucked by me or fucked over
by me. And she doesn't need to be disappointed by a 42 year old
old fart who can't fuck his way out of a paper bag: Bob Flanagan
Partypoopermasochist. Just because I'm disappointed doesn't
mean she has to be. And there's the root of my anger. Sheree
doesn't care what I'm feeling when she's stoned. She's a steam-
roller, Baby, and she rolls right over me, and it give me the blues.
I try to be rational and explain myself, I try to be funny and
laugh it off, I take the defensive mode and try to stamp out the
sparks she's igniting by continuing to drag her fingernails across
the blackboard of my psyche, but only she can prevent this for-
est fire and she has no desire for that, no, it's a raging infernod-
dddddddd... fuck it, she just bugs me when she's stoned god
dammit and I'm tired of it, and now it's tomorrow and after

another long night I'm just tired — period. Apologies all around, but what a needless waste of time and energy to begin with. Excuse me while I go check to see if Sarah came home last night so I can fuck her in the ass, eat her shit and beg her to cut my dick off and shove it down my throat.

8/24/95 Forget the jokes and the clever writing, this Sarah shit with Sheree makes me feel sad and depressed, and pissed as hell at Sheree who's of course drunk and stoned again sleeping beside me and I'm sick of the sight of her being drunk and stoned and the absolute stupid shit she says and even stupider things she thinks when she's drunk or stoned. Went to MOCA tonight with Sheree, Kirby and Sarah, and then we hooked up with Rita and had Mexican food. Through it all I was feeling good, in a happy mood, joking, laughing. Then Sarah and I came home and Sheree stayed with Rita and Kirby to get stoned and came back and it was still ok. I read back last night's journal entry to them for Kirby to tape, and it almost seemed like Sheree got what I was saying, stoned or not, it seemed like she understood why I have no interest in an 18 year old fan, that she's all I need and all I want. Anybody else would take some sort of comfort or satisfaction in that position but not screwy Sheree. And when Kirby leaves it's more of the same bullshit as last night. She doesn't get a thing. I know it's more complicated than how I'm describing it, and it probably has a lot to do with her feelings about losing me, but when conversations, stoned or not, invariably end with her telling me how bored she is, how she can't take it anymore, how we might as well split up, well what good does this do me? See? I said there wasn't going to be any clever writing here.

8/25/95 Trying to avoid head nods and finger slugs after a long day and a long week. Sitting here in bed playing computer Solitaire and sticking my nose into the internet which is boring as hell, especially when you've got a real life like mine with a day spent watching young Sarah get her pink little nipples pierced by Crystal Cross while Sheree and Kirby video tape and I hold her hand and try not to drool over those young, phlegm filled breasts, and cystic or no cystic, Sarah's got a couple of nice breasts hanging on those crappy lungs of hers. Yeah, I sound like a lech except that once again this is her wish come true, not mine. This was the highlight of her week and I'm just glad I could be of some assistance. Ever the camp counselor, ever the role model, even when it comes to helping a young girl get her tits pierced. Sure beats the hell out of making lanyards. Dinner at Figs afterwads with Molly, Murray, Richard, Ted, Ed (Smith) and Jenny (Oh, excuse me — Jennifer — the bitch). Food was great. Jennifer was not. Now we have to hear how her mother ruined her life. How all I wanted was to get rid of the kids so I could be alone with Sheree. Well, maybe that's true, but I sure did a lousy job of getting rid of them, cause they're always, even today, a cockeyed glance or a telephonic *Hello, Mom* away from making our lives a living hell. In the meantime, Sarah and her nipples are winging their way back home, and I'm glad to be home alone at last with Sheree even though she's dead to the world and I will be too, soon, in more ways than one.

8/26/95 Very very sleepy. Slept most of the day, in bed or on the couch. No magical writing tonight. Molly and Sheree are upstairs watching tv and I'm down here dozing. Maybe I'll do some more later, but for now I'm done.

8/27/95 Fun with my new parachute that Sheree bought for me at the Sunset Junction Street Fair. Five pounds for a little while on my freshly shaved balls, just like old times. I shaved my balls, how bout brushing my teeth? Why's that so hard? Same reason my penis isn't. I'm tired. I'm distracted. So Sheree's going to feed me to the dogs before I die.

8/28/95 Late again. Slept a little after hanging a five pound weight on my balls with my new parachute that Sheree bought for me at the Sunset Junction street fair. Five pounds for 30 min- ues. I enjoyed the endurance part but where's the hard-ons?

Where's the new drug, yoyobean or whatever it's called? Saw Obler today and he called in a new prescriptin for this "yoyobean' or whatever it is because he couldn't fill it. It's supposed to increase my libido. It already has I guess or I wouldn't be hanging weights on my balls till all hours of the morn.

8/29/95   No coming from the "yoyobean." Not even a hard-on. Upset stomach today to boot. Nausea and vomiting. Skipped Debbie's in favor of lying around naked watching the city fall apart via the OJ trial and racist cops and inept, underpaid city employees. I shouldn't give a shit but it is kind of depressing. It's funny after all the good writing I've done lately, suddenly I have nothing to say but blah blah blah. The daily doo doo. We have a house guest again: Linda Kauffman. Dinner at Netty's and then Kirby came over and we screened the Bobumentary for her. She had a few helpful comments. I kind of wish Sheree hadn't of gotten her stoned first, though. Don't trust that weed. And of course even without being stoned Sheree has a hard time keeping up with the processs of making work. She always wants it to be done already. And she doesn't understand that at this point no idea is sacred and everything is up for grabs or out the window. When she's stoned it's almost impossible to communicate on a serious working level. Ultimately this is Kirby's film. It's his vision. He's the one who has to drive it along and we collaborate by helping to solve whatever problems need to be solved. That's all art is: problem solving. That's why it's hard for Sheree, because she still thinks something mysterious is going on when in the end it's just 2 + 2.

8/30/95   Sheree's decorating our canopy bed with all of our SM gear; all the whips, clothespins, paddles, leather hood — surrounding us as we sleep. That's the problem: we just sleep. It all looks good and makes me feel wistful, and it even makes my dick jump a little, but I just don't have the lungs for it. My head is throbbing like a gong. What other kind of pain do I need? I look at my dick and balls (which I'm constantly fondling) and I'd like to hang some weight on them and stand around awhile, but I'd also like to stretch out here in bed and play with myself until I fall asleep. Uh oh. Now Sheree's here with her camera. It's like living with Weegee.

8/31/95 Second time around because the computer fell asleep and didn't save the short paragraph I had just completed. Sleeping, that's my job. That's all I did today was sleep. I paid my bills, but who gives a shit. So I'm a good citizen. I've already been asleep tonight but I woke up short of breath as usual. Now Sheree got me watching *Don't Look Now* but she's back to sleep, snoring of course. Earplugs in. So now it's *Don't HEAR Now*. It's 2:30 in the morning and that's about as brilliant as I get. Another month gone and I'm not, but I think about it an awful lot.

September 1995

9/1/95 Same writing spot in the same bed at the same time by the same half, make that three quarters dead, half assed, has been at the keys, tv on, people fucking, suddenly I'm not even getting hardons, I like my dick, the way it looks, the way it feels, and Sheree, she looks good to me, as do all these whips surrounding our bed, and I love my parachute and might even hang 5 pounds on my balls when I'm done here, but where's my hard ons? As a matter of fact, I AM done here. I want my balls pulled.

9/2/95 I should probably try writing during the day sometime just to get out of this rut. I should try doing something during the day. Haven't done a goddamn thing all day. Slept. Watched crap on television. Went to Debbie's. Watched the sunset from the patio with Sheree until we got into another "discussion" about how and where I'm going to die. How unfair and unsubmissive I'm being about the whole thing. She was stoned of course, the only time we ever talk about these things. I want to die in the hospital. She wants me to die at home. Can't really talk about it because if she doesn't hear what she wants she screeches and talks shit until I get pissed and she storms off or I do. It's all stupid. Takes the fun out of dying. Speaking of dying. Why won't rock and roll die? The Rock and Roll Hall of Fame concert has been on tv for what seems like a million hours and man are those fuckers old and tired and boring. "Rock and Roll will never die..." Somebody shoud definitely pull the plug. I've got to start getting some work done. I've sure got a lot of gall to waste the amount of time I waste doing nothing, but I feel like shit and nothing is all I can handle. I'll hang a weight on my balls, but that's it. And that's where I'm headed now. And another night of crappy sleep and anxious dreams. I keep dreaming I have to go back to school and take some kind of final exam so I won't flunk out, so I can still graduate. I also dreamt the house was flooded with water and I was trying to suck it out with a garden hose. Then I wake up feeling like a truck ran over my chest, and I'm spitting up bloody phlegm. Now it starts all over again.

9/3/95 Sleeping before I even start. The writing can't be anything but garbage when ijjjjjjjjjjjjjjjjjjjjjjjjjjjjjjjjjjjjjjjjjjjjjjjjjjjjjjj jjjjjjjjjjjjjjjjjjjjjjjjjjjjjjjjjjjjjjjjjjjjjjjjjjjjjjjjjjjjjjjjjjjjjjjjjjjjjj jjjjjjjjjjjjjjjjjjjjjjjjjjjjjjjjjjjjjjjjjjjjjjjjjjjjjjjjjjjjjjjjddd — see what I mean. Maybe later.

And now it's almost 5 in the morning. Nice hard-on here. Nothing was working there for a while. It seemed to get worse when I cut back on the Zoloft and started that yoyobean stuff which was supposed to help me come again. Well, not only did I not come, the hard-ons went, and sleep has been really sporadic and strange. Sheee's back to sleep, snoring. I slept for an hour here, a few minutes there, even slept with my dddddddddddddddddddddddddddddddddddddddddddddddddddddddddd dddddddddddddddddddddddddddddddddddddddddddddddddddd... oops. Fell asleep at the wheel again. What I meant to say is I fell asleep with the parachute on, and woke up to the flash of Sheree's camera. I'm sort of awake now and not feeling as bad as I did most of the day. Percocet. Also, maybe the trick is not to go to sleep, since it's waking up that feels the worst. Maybe when I do go off into a deep sleep my body thinks it's dead, and when I wake up it's like rising from the grave, and I'm a zombie all day. Isn't that the costume I was wearing when Sheree and I first met? Yeah, but I was an active little zombie then. I was a stiff who was constantly stiff. This morning Sheree lubed me up and climbed onto my peek-a-boo prick. It felt good but at that point in time the chest pains and shortness of breath were unbearable. And of course after she was done climbing on my monkey bar she wanted me to lick her while she masturbated, but I just couldn't do it, I wasn't into it — moving — I wasn't into movingjssssssssssssss ssssssssssssssssssss... oh oh... sleep perchance to fuck up. Ok, that's it.

9/4/95 Where's my head and what's inside it? Distracted by tits and fucking on television. Dumb movie that Sheree wanted to watch and now she's asleep and this crap is on to distract me. The end of the Labor Day weekend. I have to say I hate Labor Day, the way I hate all special three-day weekend days. I can't wait for Tuesday to come, when everybody else is back to work and everything is in its rightful place, tv shows where they're supposed to be, the freeway traffic flow back on schedule, offices open, answering machines off, and me on, I hope. So out of sorts physically and mentally the past couple of days. The increase in Predisone perhaps. We had a little bar-b-que soiree here tonight with Molly, Megan and John, and Kirby and Rita. I felt irritated some of the time and tried to hide it but don't think I did. Anyway the night ends with me feeling like a jerk. I was a jerk this morning when I got pissed off trying to fix the Pee Boy and took it out on Sheree, just a little flare up, but hurtful none-the-less, and stupid and abusive on my part. Hot sun, shortness of breath, headache, Prednisone and that stupid dickless wonder who won't pee where he's supposed to — all conspire to light my fuse and kaboom. But the alabaster asshole's tinkling now and all's right with the world. The flesh and blood asshole is still an asshole, a troubled young man with a permanant worry crease embedded in his forehead, right beteween the eyes. Mom was right: "You keep frowning like that and your face will stay that way forever." Before you know it I'm going to look just like that dried up apple head.

9/5/95 Should stop playing Solitaire and write something here. The sun's just rising, so I'm squeezing this entry in while it's still "night." But it doesn't mean I have anything to say. Feeling horrible lately. Doctor's tomorrow. I'm always so tired, so irritable, so long it's been good to know ya. This is just a space filler. I can't just keep writing the same complaints over and over again. I might as well go back to playing Solitaire.

9/6/95 The writing has become as dull and sleepy as I've been the past few days. Can't wake up. Headed for the hospital soon I'm sure. Doctor's tomorrow. Kirby was over today talking about the film. I got kinda pissed cause he wants John Lee to do the "Mop and Broom" illustration and Donna to do the torture machines. Naturally I want to do it all. I heard him whispering to John benind my back at our barbeque the other night. Something about my health. Something about my not being able to draw. But that's bullshit. I've got better ideas than anyone. True, whether or not I can implement them is another matter, but I'll try.

9/7/95 The full moon is setting over the dried up resevoir. I wake up again for no reason, probably because I can't breathe. Depressing day obsessing on how lousy I feel. Exhausted because I got very little sleep last night because I woke up at 3 and started watching a film about a woman who gives birth to a blood-sucking monster. Couldn't go to sleep until the damn thing came to term and then I just couldn't sleep. Been tired and achy all day. Almost called the tv station to complain about the obnoxious weatherman. I'm becoming an old cantakerous fart. Next I'll be writing letters to the editor. I told Dr. Riker how awful I've been feeling but he didn't say much. He did the steth-escope thing and said I sounded good, and we set a date for me to come into the hospital later this month, after Sheree's birth-day. It's like plannng a vacation. Club MED indeed. So what do we do about how shitty I feel? Riker doesn't say this, but the answer is: Live with it. Live with it until you die. Keep popping those Percocets as the moon sets slowly over the horizon and the green phlegm rises up my esophogus, up and out, into this glorious new day.

9/9/95 Didn't write yesterday. Forget the reason why, exhausted probably. I'm exhausted again tonight but I persevere. There's a movie on tv called 3*Some*. Laura Flynn Boyle, one of the Baldwins and some other guy. College roommate triangle with "the other guy" being gay. Good script. I'm glad something's on cause I don't want to go to sleep. I keep having these terrible attacks, last night and tonight. Mucus plugs clogging me up so bad I feel like I'm drowning. Coughing my head off. Turning blue. Eyes watering. Body drenched in sweat. It scares the shit out of me. I'll probably wind up in the hospital sooner than later, even though I "sound so good" according to people on the phone like Barbara from Geneva who called this mornng with great news: they want to use the confetti coffin in a show there next spring. That's great. Now I can go full steam ahead with the assurance that the work's going to go somewhere. Problem is I've got no steam. But I'll go ahead as far as I can go. Another reason I didn't write yesterday is I've been working hard editing and rewriting the *Pain Journal* for Cathy Busby. And now it's for me as well because it's turned into a good piece in it's own right — I think.

9/10/95 Trying to type through this 4 am headache. A bad one. A bad one, right behind the eyes and under my forehead and cheekbones. It's just bad. Took three Percocets. Waiting. Dot dot dot. Computer went into sleep mode and crashed so I put it away and commenced watching movie about a serial ax murderer who's killed in the electric chair but comes back to terrorize and kill the family of the cop who arrested him. Stupid plot but so stupid I have to see how they're going to get out of it. Here I am one more night wide awake. At least I'm not coughing. The last couple of nights I've had these awful attacks that I thought would never end. Sounds like a James Taylor song.

9/11/95 I just wait too late to write. I'm falling asleep after sleeping on the couch all day. Even canceled Dr. Obler cause I couldn't wake up or stop wheezing and coughing. Felt guilty about canceling just the same. Feel guilty about not writing and wasting so much time, but what can I do, I'm tired.

9/12/95 Typing to the sound of the tinkling Pee Boy, downstairs in bed with Sheree with the bedroom door open on a mild summer night, the television on (always), our clothes off (almost always), clean sheets, dirty dirty body (me), short of breath, headache, constant wheeze, chest muscles that tighten like rubberbands whenever I get up off the couch and try to do something like take a piss, and if I eat anything I feel bloated and heavy like a wet newspaper, simply put, I'm a wreck. Feel guilty because I can't bring myself to do anything and there's so much I want to do. At least the tv is some sort of flow of information that demands little of me. Tv and driving. Two things I enjoy because they both involve or imply movement without getting me out of breath. But now I don't even want to leave the house to drive. Skipped Obler yesterday. Skipped Debbie's tonight. I probably need to go into the hospital. I'm scheduled for the 26th, but I can't go on feeling like shit every day and wasting this much time. On the other hand I don't want to leave Sheree and this great place, our bed, our tv, our Pee Boy.

9/13/95 I knew that I'd wake up in the middle of the night to cough my head off or take a piss or both and that would give me ample oppertunity to write tonight and sure enough kkkkkkkkkkkkkk I do wake up, but look, I'm dozing nonetheless. Still unable to move my ass or activate my brain. I'm brain dead as well as physically kaput. And I fall asleep again, sitting here at the computer at 2 am.

9/14/95 I wake up with a cold. One of the worst headaches ever, clogged sinuses, sore throat. In a fog all day — again. Trying to get myself together to do something constructive but all I want to do is sleep. I can't wait to stop writing this crappy paragraph so I can get on with zoning out. The writing was so good and all of a sudden it just went poof. Sheree's bugging me cause she's so out of it.

I sat talking to her for 15 or twenty minutes on the couch until I realized she was sound asleep. I kept calling her name louder and louder and she never woke up, so I came down stairs. She finally came down and she's lying here half awake yawning and reading and scratching her butt. Tired from the long drive to Orange County to register for school. Drunk on champagne from celebrating Richard and Ted's move to the mansion on the hill. I stayed home to do work but just got up and stared at the computer every now and then waiting for something to happen. Trying to figure out how to update my mailing list in case someday I get it together to write a letter to some of the many people I owe letters to.

9/15/95 I'm mad at myself for wasting so much time, watching so much tv, sleeping so much, going back and forth to the computer and turning it on but not doing anything with it and going back to the couch and sleeping and watching the OJ trial when there's so much else I want to do: scan pictures for the confetti casket; write to Barbara in Geneva re: the confetti casket; write a bunch of letters: Kevanne; people who have faxed me re: performances; Steve Allen re: the rights to the clip we want to use for Kirby's film; a whole shit load of stuff I need to do for the film — but I just keep sleeping, wheezing and sleeping, coughing and sleeping. The writing has gotten insipid. So why don't you stop already. OK. Guess what? I'm going to sleep.

9/16/95 Another really bad night and I'm still awake (3 am). Last night I fell asleep but woke up an hour and a half later coughing and gasping for the next three hours. Tonight all I did was come downstairs afterddddddddddddd — oh, see that? NOW I'm sleeping, when I should be writing. So what I meant to say was tonight I came downstairs after sleeping most of the day on the couch and just about immediately went into a tailspin of coughing and wreching and wheezing. Finally calmed down a bit. Ready for sleep. Rita and Kirby came over to go to the movies but only Sheree went because I just couldn't get off the couchka vvvv... Maybe I should start writing during the day to avoid falling asleep on the job. With all this coughing and lethargy I'm headed for the hospital sure as shit. Thought I'd try and hold out for Sheree's birthday but enough is enough.

9/17/95 My wheezes are like little high pitched voices in my chest screaming for help, and boy do I need it. But it will probably be another day before I get to check into the hospital. In the mean time I upped my Prednisone. Slept on the couch most of the day. Molly and Sheree went out, Donna came over, Sheree went out, I slept and sweated. I did manage to finally knock off a letter to Kevanne and fax it to her in Prague. Many more things to. I do have a tad bit more energy, thanks to the Prednisone. If I thought I could stay out of the hospital until next week and not miss Sheree's birthday and get a better handle on some of the work I need to do, I'd stay out, but at this point the longer I stay out the harder it's going to be to get better.

9/18/95 *Tell me over and over again my friend you don't believe we're on the eve of* admission — admission into the hospital. My lungs are like a couple of cement mixers, churning this dark green crap, making my chest itch from the inside out. No amount of coughing is enough. I'm filling up 5 to 6 paper cups a day of pseudomonis pudding, and if I leave one of those cups unattended on the coffee table or the night stand for just an hour or so suddenly teams of disease loving ants turn their sick little antennae toward me and make an ant farm of my phlegm. Disgusting. My disease is disgusting. I'll probably miss Sheree's birthday- again. And if I didn't miss it I'd have no energy for it or anything else. Hard to squeeze in art, writing, sex, love or anything else when your whole life is consumed with dying. I'm trying to get things done, trying to give Sheree the attention SHE deserves, but I feel like I'm suspended in a vat of my own internal secretions.

9/19/95 Same time of night, different bed, different place: the hospital. Thick green phlegm, difficulty breathing, chest pains, headaches, the usual. This time I did get some Demerol. After waiting here for five hours with no orders from Dr. Riker, no food, no Percocet, no nothing but the ever-tightening pain in my back muscles, my chest and my head, only then did I get some Demerol. It really doesn't make me high or anything but it does smooth out all the pains, and that in and of itself is as good as being high. That's funny: I used to talk about *using* pain to reach an altered state: *I'm high as a kite on a drug called pain*. Well this kite has had all the wind knocked of it. Some part of me is still a masochist, but I can't fight the shortnesss of breath, well I can fight it, but in order to do that I have to surrender to it and that means move slowly, sit still, and do absolutly nothing. SM requires a certain amount of running around and a lot of mind over matter. Fuck it, I'm tired. I don't mean tired tonight and I want to go to sleep, I mean life tired. So give me some Percocet or some Demerol so at least my brain can dance a little jig. The dreaded Pain Management Team is due in to give me another anti-drug pep talk. Fuck them. Fuck everybody. My PCO2 is 64 and my PO2 is 88. The numbers keep getting worse, and lo and behold I feel worse. What a coincidence. Tomorrow I go in for surgery to put a new porta cath in my arm and take out the old one which is badly clotted. Minor surgery, but all surgery makes me nervous. What if a chunk of this clot breaks off and gives me a stroke or something? What if.

9/20/95 It's not fair to the writing that I save it up until the very last minute of the day when I can barely keep my eyes open and my brain is out the window, but it's this or nothing, so I go on, boy do I go on. They took the old porta-cath out of my chest today and put a new one in my left arm. So now both my chest and my arm are sore, especially my arm. We did some Demerol but it's not so great. Pain Management was here again, a better guy this time, more understanding, more inventive solutions including Percodan or morphine to take the place of the Percocet. So they want me to stop the Demerol. No problem, it doesn't work very long anyway, and it just makes me sweat. And suddenly I'm strangely depressed and don't know what to do with myself. The pain in my arm is bugging me. Everything bugs me. I couldn't stand talking to anyone on the phone, including Debbie and my parents. But where's Sheree? She went to Alice Wexler's for dinner, but where is she now? She hasn't called, and I'm ready to head off into sleep so I can shut the crap of the world off. Letterman. Boring. I should talk.

9/22/95 Missed a day of writing because I just dropped off the edge of the world last night, exhausted, only to wake up with a pounding head, some wheezing and coughing, and a black and blue sore arm from the new porta-cath. It's still sore, and the bruise is creeping down my arm. But it's my ticket to Demerol since the headaches are now being treated by Dilauded the *Drugstore Cowboy* drug. I don't know what the whole hub bub's about. It didn't do much for me in the altered state department, and only after increasing the dose and combining it with some other drugs did it start to stop the headache. There was a moment this afternoon when I was pleasantly floating around a little, but it hasn't happened since. And I'm starting to get a nagging irritation between the eyes like the beginnings of a headache, so there you have it. Today, by the way, is Sheree's birthday. Spent most of the day making a card for her on the computer. I took a photo of myself and implanted candles all over my back and on my head and in my ears and said "Happy Birthday, You Still Get Me Hot!." What is this writing? Just reporting. Phone calls: Tim, but I had to go because I was getting a breathing treatment; Mom, of course; Dad; Amy, from Colorado where she's visiting her brother with the brain tumor; Debbie (breathing treatment again); Ed, but I was playing Solitaire and watching *X Files*; Megan Williams, wanted to know what to get Sheree for her birthday. There's a party tomorrow at Rita's which I'll try to get to if I can escape here for awhile. So the hell with it. That's the end of this very uncreative writing.

9/23/95 A late nighter. Scott brought me back from Rita and

Kirby's at about 11:30, big red puffy face huffing and puffing because I ran out of oxygen on the way down here. Not that I was breathing all that much better even with the oxygen at the party. It was really difficult hanging out and talking to people. I couldn't wait to leave, even though it was in honor of Sheree's birthday. I didn't see much of her because she was busy getting stoned or talking to people. I don't mean for that to sound like I'm down on her for that, I'm not. I'm just saying this wasn't the time for the two of us and I had a difficult time breathing and I'm sick to death telling people how sick to death I am. Who were the people this time? Ralph Rugoff, Mike Kelley, Anita Pace, Richard Stein, Patty Podesta, Bruce Yonomoto, Ed Smith and Mio, Sumi and a spattering of also-rans. I just ain't got no party talk left in me. And I don't know nothin bout art. And, as I said, enough of me. All that's left is to shut up and do work. But that takes energy. So all that's left is to shut up and take drugs. I'm filled to the brim with pain killers but I'm still aching and paining. My arm is all athrob and my head's back to it's old tricks again, although not as bad as before. I'm just doomed. I'm getting a little bit of Demorol. But all that is is a kiss on the cheek. I want some tongue — fuck the tongue, how 'bout some dick, some analgesic dick down my throat or up my ass, makes no difference, just as long as you make like you love me and take away the pain.

9/24/95 Demmed out on Demerol at the end of September, something to remember. I keep dozing because it's two in the morning and I did just get a shot of D for the pain in my arm, but the pain persists, and there's no buzz no more no how, so I best just stop asking for the damn stuff. Aren't I supposed to be *Supermasochist*? I am according to a couple of young fans who were here this evening. Two young guys, Thad and Larry, friends of Christine's, a fellow cystic on the floor, they had a bootleg copy of *Happiness in Slavery* and couldn't believe that the famous Bob Flanagan was right here under their noses. So they asked me to sign their cd and their videotape, which of course I did, being the kindly old fart that I am: *To Thad, Bob Flanagan (the guy in the chair)*; *To Larry, Bob Flanagan (the naked guy)*. I'm always afraid these *fans*, once they meet me in the crappy flesh, are going to be rudely disappointed when they see me for the farty old phlegm bag I really am. But Thad and Larry were apparently overjoyed and we had a nice visit even though they interrupted what little wave of a Demerol rush I was getting and they made me miss the end of a really good *Seinfeld*, but such is the price of fame.

9/26/95 I choose sleeping over writing so the 25th is a blank. Even if I had written something it would have been just as blank. Just now the phone rings. It's Sheree letting me know she arrived home safely after paying me a visit on her way home from school. Again she lets loose with her plaintive whine "I just want some kind of together." I say what I always say. "I'm doing the best I can." The average cystic still dies around 29 or 30. The life span hasn't jumped for years now. As one of the doctors put it today, "They've hit a wall." At 42 I'm one of the anomalies. How can I complain? Because at 42 I feel like 62, that's how. And I've got to work 10 times harder to get 5 steps short of whereever it is I want to go. What the hell. PCO_2 yesterday was 74. Yikes! This morning it had creeped down to 70. That just means more headaches. And I can kiss my Demerol and my Percocet buzzes goodbye if I still want to breathe.

9/27/95 Yes I did kiss the Demerol good bye, and my head and arm were going wild, especially my arm. It feels like I've been stung by a bee. So tonight they gave me a shot of Benzadrine, not as much fun as Demerol, but I did fall into a deep sleep for all of an hour and a half. This pain shit is driving me nuts. Didn't accompish anything today. Played computer Solitaire and watch the OJ closing arguments all day. Problem with the closing arguments is first that they're all day long, from 9am till 8pm. But the worst part is that they demand all of your attention. You can't have it as background. You have to listen to every word. But I did fall asleep through much of of it. So not only did I not get anything done, but I still don't know what's going on. S'cuse me while I pee… my urinal is pleased. But I'm not. Phleghm is as thick and as green as ever. Short of breath. Won't say headache again but it's there. Sheree's afraid I'm going to drop off into a coma at any moment. She wants me home. I have to admit the hospital is wearing thin. But I don't want to be home either. The problem is I want to be comfortable and I'm not, no matter where I am or what I do or what I take. It makes me very anxious. And look at the effect it has on my writing. No, I can't blame everything on my declining lungs. Maybe I'm just a talentless fuck.

9/28/95 Dreamt we saw Dennis Cooper, in New York, of course, at some art affair, of course. He seemed shorter and thinner than last we saw him a year ago, also in New York. My eyes teared up as I said I was mad at him for not returning my calls. I almost said, "Dennis, I'm dying goddammit," but I resisted, knowing he would run from such chastisement, and I'd probably never see him again for another couple of years, so I hugged him and reassured him that I was only mad at him because I missed him. I hugged him and he felt bony. He seemed genuinely embarrassed for neglecting us, and I forgave him, but Sheree wasn't so amenable. She went ahead and held out her arms to embrace him but as he approached her he walked right past her. She got pissed and had a "that's-the-last-straw" look on her face, but I saw what happened. Just as Dennis was about to hug Sheree he walked around her to first shut off the blaring ghetto blaster in the corner. Sheree saw it as a snub. Dennis read Sheree's snub as bottled up anger, which of course would turn him off because even though Dennis is a rude fuck he hates to be called on it and would just as soon say "fuck you" than "excuse me." But I could see that this wasn't a snub and I explained to Dennis why Sheree thought it was and I literally grabbed each of them by the arm and pulled them together until they locked or folded or flopped into an embrace. Sheree's face over Dennis' shoulder seemed relieved to be finally making contact with the great and powerful Dennis. Dennis' face over Sheree's shoulder seemed to be wincing and saying "Christ, what I have to go through just to be Dennis."

Now it's night time. Not yet dream time, still the real world, where anxiety reigns supreme because it's still so hard to breathe and I can't enjoy my modest opiate romps because we're doing everything we can do to bring my PCO_2 down, including cutting down on the pain drugs, which is why the headaches are back, and pumping less oxygen up my nose, which is why it's so much harder to breathe and why my finger nails look like Blue Meanies and why I'm so anxious; but I'm also anxious cause Sheree just called from home after stopping to see me on her way home from Irvine: someone busted into Susan's place next door and ransacked the place. They broke the lock and came in the back door. Now we have that to worry about. Why don't they let a guy die in peace. In one piece, anyway. Tomorrow morning more blood gasses. Tomorrow afternoon big pow wow with hospital nurses and staff and Sheree to discuss the what ifs when I die. It doesn't quite seem real to me. Like it doesn't seem real that someone's going to break into our place and fuck with our stuff, but they will, no matter what we do to try and keep them out. It's only a matter of time.

9/29/95   Lots I want to write about but I'm just about to get hooked up to the bipap — yes the dreaded bipap again because I always said when I had nothing else to lose and on the off chance that it just might help, then I'll give it another try — well with today's blood gasses at PCO_2 at 69 and the PO_2 somewhere in the 80's, and feeling like shit the way I do, like I'm drowning everynight, like I've got a plastic bag on my head — we've reached that magical line of demarcation called "what the hell do I have to lose?" So I don't know how much I'm going to feel like writing with this thing sucking on my face like a mechanical squid, and there's much to not only report but to comment and reflect upon, the most important one being the meeting today with Sheree and the nurses and hospital chaplain discussing how it's going to be when I'm dead. Our frankness and love blew them away. Their nurturing and understanding put us at ease. It was a very good meeting. But for now I gotta go.

9/30/95 Hard to believe another month has done its dirty deed. Jane, Stewart and the kids, and Sheree were here for a brief visit, as was Scott W. earlier on. I told my mother on the phone the other day that I hated visiters and it sort of shocked her. I think she took it personally. Actually I don't mind brief visits. "Hi, Bob. How are you?" "Lousy. Better. Blah blah blah. Bye." "Bye." Phone calls are ok, most of the time, but visits with people sitting in those stupid chairs staring at me in my stupid bed. It makes me nervous. This coming from the guy who brought you *Visiting Hours?* Go figure. On the other hand I can't stand the thought of being neglected and forgotten. But what control do I have over that. If they remember me, they're my friends. If they don't, they're fucked. Riker consented to a little bit of Demorol, but it didn't do much for very long. Let's try it again in a couple of hours. The pain management guy is an idiot. I told him I had some serious things to confront such as my short life expectancy, and all he did was chuckle and say good bye, see you tomorrow. As far as other writing goes today, I e-mailed a letter to Deborah Drier in NY. Let's put that right here and then call it a night:

> Dear Deborah:
> How nice to get your e-mail. I've been thinking about you all week but didn't have your e-mail address with me down here — "down here" being the hospital again. I've got a new modem on my powerbook, and between e-mail and faxes it makes the visit here much more tolerable, dare I say "fun?"
> What's not fun, however, is the rude facts concerning my health. What I've felt all along since January is finally showing itself in the numbers, the stuff the doctors look at. A year of telling everybody I'm feeling lousier and lousier doesn't stack up to a couple of columns of increasing or decreasing digits. In the pul-

monary functions column I'm declining: FVC: 1.10, FEV1: 0.48. And in the blood gas department the PO2 is down (88), and, worst of all, the PCO2 is up: 69, and it keeps going up, which means they have to cut down on the oxygen (which means I can't breathe), and they have to cut the Percocet (which means more headaches — the fucking "pain doctor", when I told him, more than the pain, I can't stand the distraction of the headaches when I'm trying to do work, all he had to say was, "Well if you have a headache at least you know you're alive." And then chuckled himself out of my room. Good thing too, cause I wanted to throw something at him just to let him know that he too was still alive.) Anyway, sorry to ramble, but I know that you know, because of your own problems, the significance of all this.

But enough about me and the fact that I feel like shit and even my doctor admits I've probably got about a year to live, if I'm lucky, how the hell are you, Deborah? How are your lungs, and your numbers? And how's your work? As far as Mr. Silverberg goes, these are screwy (fuck it — downright immoral!) people. He and David were good friends of ours, like family. Except for being possibly absent-mindedly rude once or twice, Sheree and I did nothing wrong to these two jerks, and yet we've been totally cut off for the past two years, and it hurts like hell even now. I had a dream about Dennis Cooper, personal friend of Mr. Silverjerk, and (I thought) very close friend of mine, and there have been no problems between us, but Dennis too hasn't returned my calls. Early on Jane Goodall talked about chimps who got sick and were ostracized by the rest of the group and left to die. Excuse me while I ring the nurse for a couple of bananas.

Enough with the complaints. I forgive them all. Dying is just yucky.

Re: reading in November, of course Sheree would love to be in NY in November, especially around Halloween, our anniversary, but a lot depends on her MFA show, and how I'm feeling. Also I'll only do it if we could generate a pretty good sized crowd on such short notice and there would be some way of paying for the trip. I'm not familiar with Hearns, so maybe I should talk to him. Is Artforum really hanging you up on this event thing? How bout dying? Can we make that into an event? (Obviously I've got a one tracked mind these days). Something else to consider: Galerie Analix in Geneva has invited me to show my new *Dust to Dust* casket piece in the spring of 96. Not sure yet if it's a one man show or a group show, but it will be an event.

Again, I hope your lungs are holding out. E-mail me if you can while I'm here a'lopital since I don't have OJ to pass the days anymore. I'm including my "Dennis" dream and another piece that I like a lot. Hope you enjoy them. And let me see what you've got cooking. Sheree sends her love as well.

And that's it for September. Now before midnight tomorrow I have to fill out this Gugenheim grant and get my slides in order, write up a proposal, and talk Sheree through the computer to print things out — all for a measily 40 thousand dollars.

10/1/95 How can I stand it, punching into this laptop in my lap after a horrendous day of digital dementia and frustration. The Guggenheim application is due by midnight tonight, twenty minutes from now. Most of the day was spent on the fucking information highway like a stray dog bounding in and out of traffic, talking to Sheree on the phone trying to talk her through the Mac at home so I can put together my Googie package, but it's like trying to teach her to fly a space ship over the phone, and I'm not that great an astronaut myself to know all the answers plus I'm not even through with writing the proposal for the Googies, and I hate it when I get Sheree so frustrated she starts crying. So fuck it. She came down and took what I had to send and is now, I hope, at the post office,and I hope not too frazzled. I'll just have to e-mail the Googies my note explaining that I'm a sick little snot and the dog ate my artwork. Meanwhile here's Dr. D. Last call for Demerol so by morning it won't be knocking my PCO2 into the stratosphere. Between Demerol, Dilaudid, Feurocet, Theodur and Prednisone my kettle of pharmaceutical soup is foaming up to a rapid boil. Now if only the rest of the world and their fucking computers would just keep up with me.

10/2/95 A day of big news: I took a shower! And the OJ jury has reached a verdict in only 5 hours. Won't know what it is until tomorrow. It will definiately be *The Day the Earth Stood Still* tomorrow morning when the verdict is announced. But bigger news than that is my PCO2 is down to 57! "Rumors of your demise have been greatly exagerated," says Dr. Riker. "You're squeezing every last drop of life out of me like a lemon," I say. What caused the improvement? Antibiotics, Prednisone, Bipap, DNase, cut down in narcotics hours before drawing blood, and a reduction in oxygen too. But I'm still here in the hospital until Friday so we can get the home antibiotics (and opiates?) together, as well as the home bipap, which I intend to fashion into a leather hood just as soon as I can so I don't look like I'm wearing a jock strap on my head all night and I have something sexy looking to go with my new hard-ons that this increase in respiratory support seeems to encourage. But aside from the fun and good news I'm still tearing my hair out getting the Gugenheim material together. Went over the slides with Sheree tonight. Been trying to write my bio all day. Feels like homework. Much more to do, but I'm done for the day. Hate the Letterman show tonight because from the sound of his monologue it must of been recorded last week because his OJ jokes were banking on the assumption that the jury was still deliberating. Old news already. Old jokes. Fuck the old stuff. I'm a now kind of guy. And now I'm going. Hey, why hasn't Sheree called? I worry.

10/3/95 My brother John's birthday but I can't get through to him (so what else is new?). I mean I can't reach him by phone. So the day departs without my heartfelt sentiment. And what a weird day. OJ Day. He's free. Diddle dee dee. And aliens came down from space and mutilated a couple of humans in Brentwood last year as a change of pace from the usual desert cattle, and instead of the fancy crop circles they left us the equally mysterious Bruno Magli shoe print (size 12) and the bloody glove. What the hell were we thinking. How could we blame OJ? Meanwhile I'm here in my part of the earth still trying to get this Googie Grant proposal shit together and winding up in computer hell over the phone trying to get Sheree to print it out for me at home. I've e-mailed Ed to come to the rescue tomorrow. I hope. Now Letterman (not so funny), my snack (yum), and the scum sucking Bipap (hey, if the Bipap is a scum sucker, what does that make me?)

10/4/95 Still working all the live long day on this god damn Guggenheim Aplication. Am I lame or is it really this difficult? So I still haven't sent the fucker out and who knows, by time they get it maybe they'll refuse it, hospital or no hospital, dying genius or not. Getting Demerol every six hours or so, headaches or not. No, I had some pretty bad head pounders today, but then again am I exaggerating and sucking up to Lord Demerol? Trying to stay in his good graces so he'll shoot his warm buttery sauce all over my throbbing sinapses. Hey, there's more OJ stuff on tv. It will soon settle in to one long murder mystery we will never know the real truth abbout, like Jack the Ripper and JFK. I think I'll OD on OJ, and have some Demorol early so it will leave my system in enough time so as not to affect my blood gasses tomorrow morning. But for now I've had it with this fucking computer.

10/5/95 Demon Demerol. Damn em all. Was all set to go home tomorrow. PFT's improved since last time. Blood gasses: PCO2 55 an PO2 81. Much better. My norm. But I'm not going home yet, although Dr. Riker doesn't know it yet. With all the new pain meds, the new infusion pump, and the bipap I'm freaking out about having to do it all myself and feed myself and wipe my own butt all weekend with Sheree out of town. So I'm waiting until next Tuesday when she gets back. I feel like a jerk about it, but I'm just not in any rush to get stressed out. Just got over one major stress getting this Guggenheim together by proxy, but that's done now and all I have to do is sit back and wait for the $40,000 to roll in. The headaches are hitting me again like a 2x4 and the pain guy says he doesn't believe in IV narcotics unless the patient only has a few days to live. I can't believe I want Demerol so bad that I would exaggerate these headaches just to get a buzz. The buzz is a nice side affect but it's the headache I can't stand. I just had an infusion of D an hour ago and already I feel like somebody pushing their thumbs through my eyes and into the back of my head. But unfortunately I have more than a few days to live, so that's it for Demerol.

10/6/95 My little hospital room — still here — and I'll be here till Tuesday when Sheree comes to get me. Right now She's in Portland. Kevanne's coming to our place tomorrow. I could have gone home and spent the weekend with her but I was too overwhelmed with all the new shit I had to go home with, the bipap, the new IV pump, the new pain meds, getting off the old pain meds, no more shots of Damitall; plus, although my lung functions have shown improvement since getting here, I still feel like shit and am completely out of breath while doing the simplest things like, taking a shit or shaving. So here I be, waiting for my next shot. Waiting for the nurse to come on who pushes the Demerol, rather than the one who slowly infuses it with the pump. Fuck the pump. Gimmie the push. So what, a 30 second brain rush, is that gonna kill me? With the pump, by the time it's infused I'm wanting it again. Ah, fuck it. Why don't I just start shooting heroin like the rest of the junkies? Because I'm still a good boy. A sick boy, but a good boy. And the worst I'll do is, while the nurse is out of the room I'll take the Damitall out of the pump and give it a little push. Weeeeee! Like jumping into a nice warm pool. Make no mistake, it's a tiny push, and a tiny pool. It's no fucking diving board and I'm certainly not jumping off the roof or anything. But I'll give myself a couple of pushes here and there, and take a leap now and then, the "pain" doctor be damned. Weeeeeeee!

10/7/95 Sandwich crumbs in my bed. Pain in my head. Someday I'll be dead. Kevanne was was here today and Scott W. Now Kevanne's at our place and my head's pounding. Should cut back on the Demerol but it works. Should write about the dream I had last night that Sheree was wanted for murdering some guy, someplace near Dodger stadium, and I was somewhat concerned that the cops would think I was an accomplice because I helped her take care of the body after she killed him. But now I'm dying with this headache and I'm too tired to write. I wrote this dopey e-mail note to Ed Smith earlier today. Here it is:

My dear Mr. Smith, or HoneyToro, or Tori Spelling, or whatever the hell your name is:

Re: our phone conversation on the evening of October 6, the year of our Lord, 1995: I feel I must reiterate to you that on the subject of sadomasochism, dominance, submission, control and the sexuality and duality thereof as it pertains to myself and my partner and once and future Dominatrix, Sheree Rose, upon further reflection on my part I must again express to you my observation that you don't know jack shit, and that your head is so far up your anal cavity it's a wonder you can breathe. Not only is your argument vacuous but there appear to be more holes in your head than there are in this infamous virgin padlocked penis of which you are so proud. To enrich your education on the subject I recommend reading *Fuck Journal* (Hanuman Books, 1987), as well as the Bob Flanagan literary journals you are taking such an interminable amount of time transcribing. For your edification, when one, such as myself, commits every fiber of one's being to an S&M lifestyle, as opposed to you weekend (weak end) dabblers, one cannot expect, nor would one desire constant erections with every s&m act, since life itself becomes an s&m act in and of itself. Besides that, when one is as devoted a slave, as i indeed was (notice the lower case "i") the psychological commitment to the top and the sole desire to please the top is the number one concern. This obsession on the erection is banal, and, to be quite honest, truly boring. And as far as this issue of control is concerned, self-control is the ultimate discipline, as long as one knows the difference between controlling one's self and controlling others. Apparently you do not. However, despite your ignorance on these and many other subjects, I nonetheless find your company tolerable and amusing, so you may feel free to call me at any time.

Yours, I'm Sure,
BFSM

10/8/95 Rather than wait until the day is done and I am too spent to write anything worthwhile, how about I give it a go now, after just finishing my dinner of "Crispy Oven Chicken and Baked Beans" and having just received a shot of hot digity Demerol in my butt. Yes, a shot. The headaches have been a bitch today, so Dr. Libby, Riker's stand in this week, bumped me up to 75 units instead of 50 as a one time deal and in the muscle, not the IV. At first I was disappointed cause the IV is such a rush, but the truth is its effects disappear too quickly and all I am is a sweaty shaky guy still with a pounding head, counting the hours till my next push. But the shot in the butt has a timed release effect. So we're giving it a shot, so to speak, with the normal 50 mg. Starting to get that soft in the head feeling. Like my head's still clanging but someone's put a pillow over it so it's not so loud. Hmm, not bad. Now if I could get a shot AND a push... who needs the pain management team. I don't want to be on any fucking team. Sheree just called from Portland. Some mixup with Mollie cause Sheree's doing her leather convention thing and Mollie seems to be left in the lurch. Sheree does love her conventions. Maybe she should become a Shriner. Sheree the Shriner.

10/9/95 My last night here, I suppose, me of the exploding head, dandruff head, maybe it's all that snow that's weighing me down and making my insides pound, making me beg for the pain killer rush even though it's practically over before it even starts, although, thanks to Riker's sub, Dr. Libby Libby Libby, I got a couple of shots of 75 mg Demerol during the worst of the head storms, but then they just come back again, and the stupid pain in the ass pain doctor, Dr. Jerkass, says I'm on all the narcotics he can give me, and he looks at my profile and says he doesn't see any swollen veins, and he doesn't think superior vena cava is the right diagnosis, but I wonder where the hell he got his x-ray vision from to see the veins INSIDE my head pounding so hard I can take my pulse just by sitting here and counting the pulsations between my eyes, and any ass but Dr. Jerkass can take a look at the rigatoni-sized veins running all over my stomach and chest and know there must be something weird cooking inside my head as well, but fuck it, I'm going home, no Demerol, just the Dilaudid, which I'm not so delighted with, but as Robin, the cool nurse, said today, commiserating with me, "You're a strong man, Flanagan," yeah, tell that to Dr. Jerkass. So I'm going home tomorrow. Sheree's home and was in a great mood but there was some falling out up in Portland with Molly. Molly let loose with a tirade of hatred and bigotry toward the SM people that Sheree was spending her time with. "Those people are sick! They cut themselves and fist each other" Where the hell has she been? The world out there is as weird and as contrary and as hurtful as the veins in my head. Amtrak train derailed by a right wing group called "The Sons of Gestapo." 7.5 earthquake in Mexico. OJ OJ OJ. Fuck the world. If there's no Demerol for me, then there's no Demerol for the rest of the world either, so everybody suffers.

10/10/95 Honey, I'm home. In bed next to the warm and fleshy Sheree, who's thrilled that I'm alive after starting off the day waking from a dream that I was dead, so vivid that she called me at the hospital just as I was getting my needle changed on one arm, and blood drawn on the other, and a breathing treatment in between, so when Jesus, the respiratory therapist, answers the phone, and she doesn't hear my voice, of course it's pretty scary. Imagine how scared she would have been if she knew the guy answering the phone was named Jesus. But, no I'm not dead and I'm not with Jesus. I'm home, which is a nice stand-in for heaven, given the touch of hell I have to go through with all the new shit and headaches and shortness of breath and on and on with the complaints. The new IV's, always connected, so I only have to mess with them once a day, but I've also got to carry the damn thing around with me wherever I go, that and the oxygen. And at night I'm supposed to connect up to the bicrap dork machine, but not tonight, too much else to do. And drugs! Practically something to swallow every hour round the clock. Now that they've come up with a machine to pump the antibiotics into my veins round the clock, what about something that will automatically shove the shit down my throat?

10/11/95 It's oh so late and the bad news is I fell asleep without writing after taking an Oxazipan cause I was so anxious trying to deal with the new drug system, Jenny being a shit to Sheree on the phone, which pisses me off, but Sheree handles it well, the way she handles everything well these days, including me (I just told her she's a highly evolved person and that I love her), Ed pisses me off on the phone, calling me a control freak and spouting his stupid and cliché observations on SM that the bottom controls the top, blah blah blah, more fuel for my headache which, by the way, at 3:30 in the fucking morning right now, is the reason I'm even writing this: I come to bed at 11:30, I do a breathing treatment, I set up the new bicrap, and I fall asleep like a good boy — but son of a bitch I wake up at 1:30 with not just a headache, but this excruciating pounding hammers and nails inside my skull; I rip the fucking bicrap jock strap off my face; I'm screaming; I'm crying; I wake Sheree up; she's scared to death; "Take Percocet, take Percocet"; "No!"' and then the goddamn pump is beeping, an occlusion, something wrong with the line; I scream at Sheree to get me a needle and stuff to clear the line; does this have anything to do with the awful stuff going on upstairs? Don't know; but I'm crying and trying to dial the home care nurse; I do take the Percocet, 3 at first and then another one; and I don't know if I misdialed or what but the home care nurse never called me back; but the Percocet finally did kick in, so much so that I can barely keep awake to write this, and I managed to flush my line and get the pump to stop beeping, but I still don't know the cause of the headache — the worst one I've ever had, the worst pain I've ever had, SM, root canal, you name it — whatever, was it the occlusion? The bibap? Or a continuation and escalation of the headaches I've been having these past months? Don't know. Don't care. I'm done. That's the good news: I woke up and wrote something and didn't miss a day. Oh joy.

10/12/95 The safety of my bed. The pounding in my head. I could be dead instead. But I'm here, trying to find words to describe these horrendous 24 hours. A full blown riot in my cerebellum. My eyes in a perpetual squint. A crease like a surgical incision right btween my eyes. My mother used to say don't frown so much, the lines in your face will stay like that. And here they are. Along with — plenty of reason to frown. On the phone all morning cause the pump keeps beeping: *occlusion.* Something to do with the coinciding massive headaches? Maybe. Concluded that the drugs were programmed to pump too fast and it was too much for the poor Superior Vena Cava Boy. So they came out with a new pump and that's changed and the worst of the headaches seem somewhat gone but creeping on. And just as I was gathering together my life support systems so I could come to bed, ready to meet any emergency, I notice I'm really short of breath. I notice I can't breathe. I notice I'm out of oxygen. Completely out of oxygen. The meter says 4, but the tank's got zip. So I yell to Sheree downstairs to stay calm but come upstairs and get me my E tanks, which she does. They should last me till morning when the refills come — I hope. Now Sheree's asleep and snoring. Hate to cut off my sense of hearing, but I have to. Too nervous to listen to anybody's rattle but my own, and even that, even my own sounds make me want to slam my head into wall. But Dr. Bob has added Oxazepam to his drug regime to help him dream. Tomorrow: more oxygen; more headaches; more friends: Kirby & Rita for breakfast. Amy was here this morning, eating lox and watching my head throb and my eyes sqint like Clint Eastwood's. I have to ask myself, Do I feel lucky? Yeah sure. I ragged on David and Ira and Dennis mostly, how abandoned I feel by them now that life is getting so much harder. Dennis I can forgive, because that's always been his weird quirk, distance;

but he's always been glad to talk to me when I do call, but I won't call, not unless he does first. I determined that Dennis is inconsiderate, but David and Ira are immoral. And you can lump A.J. and most of the New York lit scene in with them. Funny, the art scene which you would think would be much shittier have treated us with much more openness and respect. They seem much more friendly and and concerned about me: John Miller and Aura Rosenberg; Mike and Anita; Julia Sher; Ralph Rugoff, to name a few. I don't have to talk to them every day, but they truly seem to care, and there's no bullshit between us. Fuck the bleeding heart poets. Yuck! I keep thinking of a line from James Schuyler (or Jimmy as they called him), the ultimate sick crazy poet who during his final days had a coterie of has beens, near-do-wells, and hope-to-be's (all of which apply to David by the way)—Jimmy had them all waiting on him hand and foot, feuding with each other over who was gonna be the best and the brightest to kiss the fruitcake's fat dying ass. But the best line of Schuyler's I keep thinking about is the last line from his hospital poems in *Morning of the Poem*: "The friends who come to see you, and the friends who don't." Fuck them all (that's my line). Obviously I ain't no Schuyler, and I've got no butt for them to kiss.

10/13/95 I'm a liar. A sleepy liar. An anal sleepy liar. Cause it's no longer the 13th. I'm waking up in the early morning light of the next day after a night anxiety over my first excursion out, the movies, *To Die For*, with Kirby, Rita, Sheree and Kevanne. Oxygen, the pump, breathing, wheelchair or no wheelchair, geting there on time so I don't have to rush, so much to consider, so much to freak out about and get shitty about and feel bad about getting shitty about. I forget to start the recorder for Sheree, so halfway through the movie I realize I'm not taping *X Files* so I feel shittier and stupid. But worse than that, toward the end of the film I notice I'm out of oxygen, stupid tank. But I stay remarkably calm. That's the key to running out of oxygen: staying calm, something I'm not always so good at but I'm surprised at how calm I was and how much I was able to breathe without the life support system last night I and was able to stay cool until we got home and I got the fresh O2 shoved up my nose and read some of the new writing to Rita and Kirby before Sheree drove them home and brought back tacos and I took an Oxazamap and bam, I'm out of it, and before I know it it's 6:30 a.m. the next day and Hello Pee Boy.

10/14/95 Early to bed to watch tv, Dana Carvey, the new *Mad Magazine* show. It's all supposed to be funny, but is it? I'm supposed to be getting better, but am I? Woke up with a pounding head and took Percocet but I'm trying not to take too much Percocet because I want to report to Riker on the drugs they gave me so they'll know whether they work or not. I've been nervous and depressed all day. Oxazipan makes me sleepy. Slept through Burt Lancaster in *The Swimmer*, watching tv with Donna and Sheree. All my life I've slept through *The Swimmer* whenever it's been on tv. Somebody better wake Donna up. Jeffrey and she are still fighting like crazy and adding more and more therepy to their days. And now they're starting to hit each other. Oh, boy. Oh no. OJ.

10/16/95 In a bad mood and getting badder. Taking it out on Sheree. That's what she gets for being there. I want her close but I can't stop the nastiness. It isn't her. It's just how I am when I'm depressed. And I am depressed. Started with the Holly Hunter interview. Excuse me while I put ear plugs in cause Sheree's asleep and breathing heavy and that really bugs me cause I want her up and talking to me and watching tv with me now that it's one in the mornning and I'm awake and *The Picture of Dorian Gray* is on tv after she came down and woke me up after I left her upstairs sleeping on the couch after her long day long drive home from Irvine — but never mind that — I was pissed that she wasn't watching a tv show about murder in our own Rampart district and then some dumb movie about a terminator substitute teacher blowing kids away while she snored away and I had a bunch of things I wanted to tell her but it wasn't only that she was asleep, I was depressed and out of breath and could barely talk anyway, but I stormed away with my stupid fashion pack drug pump slung over my shoulder like a huffy bitch, short of breath and with a headache like a penned up rodeo horse trying to kick its way out of my head — everyone who's critical of my nastiness: put a plastic bag on your head all day and every couple of hours slam your head into the coffee table and press your thumbs into your eye sockets until your eyeballs squish like bloody grapes and then tell me what a great mood you're in. And then watch your whole career blossom in front of your throbbing shriveled up eyes knowing full well that even as it's happning it's all past tense for you, with the emphasis on tense. So as Sheree, sweet Sheree, sleeps a sleep she richly deserves, unencumberd by the nastiness of the prick beside her, and the portrait of pretty boy Dorian Gray putrifies for what reason I've yet to understand, I'll continue my night time routine, sleep, wake, sleep, wake, sip water, take pills, up and down like a hamster on the wheel. A dying hamster. I guess that's better than a dead fish flushed down the toilet.

10/17/95 Strange sleeping/non sleeping habits. Go to sleep like a normal person at midnight or so, but keep waking up with awful headaches and loud wheezing, coughing up phlegm and blood; fall back to sleep and repeat the same. Sheree wakes up several times to kiss me and tell me she loves me and to remind me not to die. But, as they say, I don't know. Life is my full time job, and the pay stinks. I feel like a prisoner on the rock pile, pounding big rocks into small. Not only is there no pay, but I'm beginning to wonder what's it all for, is it even worth it. Here's where I think the advantages of IV pain meds at home would greatly outweigh the dangers. At the rate I'm going I'm at a much higher risk of saying fuck it all. I need some damitall type of spark to smoothe out the rough edges so I can devote some time and energy to something else besides the constant body maintenance and the huge effort it takes to do something as simple as trying to get a decent night's sleep or getting up off the couch to take a shit without feeling like I just ran the fucking marathon..

10/18/95 Wedding party, no, engagement party for Sheree and me at a Beyond Baroque type of place but it has all kinds of hidden hallways and trap doors/ I keep leaving the party and wind up wandering the hallways/ sexy black woman keeps showing up, running away, afraid, in a sweat/ OJ's voice in the background screaming at her/ like a movie set or a cheap carnival fun house, the walls aren't real and eventually every door leads back to Beyond Baroque where, each time I go back the crowd has grown: workshop people, Vale/ at first I was afraid there would be a terrible turn-out, but I look at the clock. The party was called for 7:30 and it was only 7:40, so it was early yet, but it was too quiet/ in the corner, on the floor, is a whole bank of tape machines and speakers but neither I nor Sheree have any tapes. I'm wondering if Dennis will show up with tapes. But after one of my returns from my hallway wanderings the crowd and the music has improved / I think Ramin brought some tapes/ it's starting to look like a real party, including a long parade of elephants with a special seat for Sheree and me...there was an earlier dream with me fighting with my parents and Tim about my death/ kitchen table from the Costa Mesa house/ something about drugs/ something about giving up.

A little less than 24 hour later, before the dreams swoop in, before the electrodes are attached to the rivets in my skull and the juice is turned on, it's time for tonight's reportage. It's bon voyage to Kevanne. As important and as supportive as she has been since the Beyond Baroque days, the old adage about fish and houseguests is certainly true, after two days the place is starting to stink a bit. Give us another day together and I think there would be some serious yelling going on. Poor Sheree got the brunt of it, which pisses me off cause she's already bearing the brunt of me, she shouldn't have to waste so much of her time driving Miss Crazy, Kevanne KooKooWood. Everyone who stays in this house should take care of me, should put my needs first and Sheree's needs first. I have enough to freak out over, and if I maintain then I don't need houseguests freaking out. I thought I would hire Kevanne as a live-in assistant but I was as nuts as

she is to come up with such a thing.. HAVE TO GET SOME
SLEEP. I'll add more later when/ if I wake up... I have awakened
5:30 am. Kevanne is gone, in tears because she's afraid she may
never see me again, which is probably true, but she hardly saw
me while she was here with her days so jam packed with anxiety.
I feel a little guilty calling her KooKooWood, and Kevanne
would be apalled, but when the computer speaks, I must write.
Let the friends and associates of Bob beware, they may wind up
here, warts and all. If I have to endure the microchip taken to
my warts and wounds, then unfortunately, by proximity, so do
they. *So I is sorry, Miss Crazy, ifn I said somfin to makes you upset
any mo den you wuz when you wuz here, but you see, it's just my
joinal and it's like the devil and sometimes I just gots ta do it. An
besides, Miss Crazy, by da time you reads this here joinal note, ifen
you do, I most surely is dead, but you can come and spit on my grave
iffen you has a needs to, I won't hold it against you cause I just ain't
here no mo.*

10/19/95 Bed. Guests gone. Christine on a bus to her boyfriend.
I sign one of my Jesus Penis cards to her: "Christine, Like your
namesake we're glad you were here and can't wait for you to
come back." Saw Dr. Riker today with my bevy of complaints.
Many tests. Results tomorrow. A quiet day, I hope. I'm passing
out as I lie here. Sheree's home from Club Utero. Now I gotta go.
I'll probably wake up several times during the night, during
which I'll maybe write some better stuff than this... and here I
am again, 5 am, splitting head- I can't say the word h-e-a-d-a-c-
h-e again. Let me just say ouch. I'm awake. The news is in my
headphones. They're fucking with medicare. Fucking with people's heads and ultimately their lives but no one cares, and in a
sense neither do I. Speaking of houseguests, I feel like my bags
are packed, I've got my ticket and I'm just waiting to leave this
crazy place I've been visiting and the nuts I've been living with
who are getting nuttier everyday, but fuck it — I'm out of here.

10/22/95 Missed the past two nights writing, partly due to exhaustion. Exhuasted again tonight but I'm plugging away at it. Sheree keeps waking up and falling asleep too but as soon as I start typing she starts snoring so in go the eargplugs. We're not fighting but I have to admit I'm still pissed at what she did to me night before last, which is partly why there's not writing there. Cutting out all the bull shit, aaaldssssssssssssssjjjjjjjjjjjjjjjjjjjjjjjjjjjj jjjjjjjjjjjjjjjjjjjjjj

10/23/95 my sister's funeral/ i'm designing the headstone/ I'm making it out of old doll parts and foam rubber/ i think it would be beautiful and poignent to have a little doll's hand come out of the headstone, rotating with the wind, 4 positions, each position a different meaning: 1. shaking hands., 2: hand extended, palm upward, like a beggar's hand., 3: I don't remember the meaning of this position. 4: wave good bye. I'm excited by all this but not sure how to make it. Get help from Jim Stoia, high school art teacher. He's not surprised to see me even though it's been 20 years. Bastard. I need glue. He's not sure where it is. The glue lady has gone home. I make some remark about Tish and I having a combined funeral but somehow I got a retreive; There's hospital where Tish spent her last days

Depressed. Not so much my health this time. Sheree. My head's still reeling from our little art "discussion" two nights ago. The usual: I'm sound asleep, if you call sucking air like a dying blow fish sound. Sheree up all night for some reason. She's video taping me as I mumble and talk in my sleep. Long story shortened: she wakes me up, she's stoned but denies it, asks if she can tell me her latest idea, I say I'd rather wait until tomorrow. Doesn't work. This is 5 a.m. By 7 I am a basket case and she has once again threatened to split up, accused me of yelling and screaming (which I never did), accused me of not helping her on her UCI show or anything else (lies), she jumped from one idea after another like freezing my head when I die, like why aren't you submissive anymore, and the topper, "How many degrees do you have?" after I gave her the asked-for advice about her thesis show in Irvine. I made the made the mistake of injecting the work "simple" as in "It's simple." Talk about yelling. "How many college degrees do you have?" The good news in this sad but familiar tale is that she had the video camera trained on me for the whole two hours of this unsolicited and non-consenting abuse. As far as I'm concerned she's no different than a drunken husband who starts bad mouthing his wife or maybe even hitting her a few times, and then in the morning everything's supposed to be ok cause it was just the alcohol talking. I looked at the video tape tonight while Sheree was at school. My thought was to transcribe it and insert it in place of the journal entry I would have been writing at that time. I never said a bad thing to her on that tape. I stayed calm in spite of the fact that I was backed into a corner over and over again and was totally exhausted and frustrated. But that's not the worst part. I could accept these little uproars and allow them to pass if they ended when the drugs ended, but they don't. As far as Sheree's concerned that night *I* was the brute. *I* was unsupportive. *I* was the one who was yelling. But it was all her. And there's no way out. If I tell her I'm upset about what I saw she'll pull the let's split up bit again. She'll say we're not compatible. She'll say she's a terrible person. All I want her to say is that she's sorry. I know the pressure she's under, but I also know this kind of post-pot insanity is nothing new. Pot screws her up and she won't admit it. She's insecure and she turns to me and she blames me at the same time. I love her. I don't want to fight with her. I'm abusive sometimes when I'm really frustrated but I can always be reasoned with and I always apologize and try to be better next time. But this shit with Sheree's been going on for years and seems to be getting worse. She's been great to me and takes great care of me, and I've always helped her and continue to help her in every way I'm still able, but why do I have to endure that pot shit? It's so useless. Such a waste of time.

10/24/95 Tried the bipap again tonight for a couple of hours but still woke up after two hours with the headache. Bipap off now. That was 2 a.m. Now it's 4. Not sure where the last two hours went. Did I fall back to sleep? Don't feel like I did. Headache better, and then worse, and then better again. Have to see the pain doctors at UCLA before anyone even thinks about giving me something stronger than Percocet or Dilaudid, both of which work a little but not enough. And what is enough? Went to the doctor's again today and again Sheree pounced on me about their unwillingness to prescribe morphine. I keep telling her it's not that easy but she gets more and more frustrated and yells at me about it. I told her about the video tape, by the way, but she remains unconvinced that I am anything but a louse and in order to maintain that position she refuses to view the tape herself. Kirby's passively pissed that I didn't wait to view the tape in his presence so he could record my reaction. Fuck him. Fuck them all. I haven't done anything wrong to anybody, not even myself. And I'm tired of being the bad guy just because I'm not who or what I used to be. Nobody misses me more than me.

10/25/95 Bicrap again for awhile but up again, 3:30 am, with the h word and the d word, depression. Now, of course, I'm falling asleep. I'm going to stop, take some Dilaudid and sleep and finish this later. Peter and Susan came over to talk about what we're doing on Saturday for the computer nerds. They like what we're doing. Never hurts to have the art critic from the *L.A. Times* on your side. Besides that I'm a wreck. Sleep all day. Up like this during the night, squinting through one eye in a feeble attempt to focus, but my only focus now is to take a piss into my bedside urinal and fall asleep... Here I am, back again, 5 am, the same pattern night after night. Just remembering a dream: Finally made it over to Ed Smith's new apartment, but I can't maneuver the stairs so I don't see the inside, and I tell Ed, as a joke, "Next time you rent an apartment, don't be so selfish, think about me." There was more to the dream. The foreign apartment manager eyes me suspiciously as I slowly try to ascend the stairs, huffing and puffing. I huff and puff more conspicuously so that he and his wife will notice I'm having trouble breathing. They bring out this strange ladder with a crank so I think they're going to help me but it's just some kind of elaborate barbeque and they go about their business and ignore me. Somehow I do see Ed's apartment and like most things in Ed's life it's not as interesting or as beautiful as he seems to think it is. But then I notice a woman in a red negligee and pierces being led by a chain to the nipples by a dominatrix and I'm very jealous and I want to cry, the way I want to in real life listening to him and his stupid Mio stories. He who couldn't care less what Sheree and I were doing 12 years ago when everybody thought we were nuts, now I have to listen to his minor spanking tales and padlock problems and watch the rest of the dumb fucks with "more holes than Swiss cheese" go from talk show to talk show, talking about their Mistresses this and their slaves that while I carry this drug pump and oxygen tubing around the house like a ball and chain, as unsexy as you can get no matter how famous I am for sensualizing the whole lot of it, I'm watching myself shrivel up, and what's worse, I'm forcing Sheree to watch it and live it, while we both pine away for the old days. This constant nausea I've been feeling lately has nothing to do with physiology, it's just me being sick to death of me and what I've become.

10/27/95 Tops on my worry chart at the moment is wondering where Sheree is. She went to Monica's annual pumpkin carving soiree, and I of course did not want to leave the house, but she called about 3 hours ago and I thought she was going to be coming home soon. Do I make myself look like a jerk and call Monica's? I'll wait a bit. Watch Letterman. Contemplate my headache which has been a terror mostly but subdued for the past few hours. So sick and so tired last night I couldn't bring myself to write anything. So now I'm awake. Now I'm writing. And where's Sheree. I'm eyeing the red light of the electronic security system. When it turns green I know she's safely home and the door is shut and I can turn toward other matters. But what if it stays red? Later on the light's still red but I made the call to Monica's and Sheree's still there, so I can relax, if that's possible with the factory of pain firing up behind my eyes, working its way down my neck muscles and ringing them like wet towels. *Raising Arizona* ending as *Broadcast News* is about to start. It must be Holly Hunter night. My fan. While I'm adding up my bodily dysfunctions, let me also say that I came this morning, the first come in over a year, as far as I can remember. I had to use the vibrator and almost lost the hard-on a few times, and it took a heavy dose of castration fantasies, but I got to the point of no return where I could sit back, huff and puff, vibrate, relax and enjoy the come, which was just about to come when the phone rang, which, thank God, Sheree answered, it was Rita who was on her way over to retrieve her slides, just as I was about to shoot, or squirt, or dribble, or whatever the hell I do, for the first time in what seems like years, but even Rita's phone call doesn't deter me, I'm strapped to a table and, without anasthesia, Sheree or somebody is cutting my dick and balls off as a keepsake after I die, something I not only fantasize about now, while I'm in the throes of orgasm, but also dreamt about the night before: Sheree and I fighting because all of a sudden she doesn't want my dick cut off and I do, but now I'm awake, and Sheree plugs in the vibrator for me, and Sheree answers the phone for me, and yes, there it is not just an orgasm, not just a shudder, not just the vibrator being turned off in frustration, but, hey a couple of drops of sperm, white stuff, but when it's all said and done, and the hard-on's gone, and the come drops dry on my stomach, the headache comes slamming on big time and stays with me bad the rest of the day, but no Dr. Jerkass says, at least I know I'm alive.

10/28/95 Crazy murder and mayhem movie on tv. *Psycho Cop 2*. Blood and tits. It's 5 in the morning again, 4 with the clocks turned back. Don't know what I'm doing up watching it. Tits are always fun, although totally demeaning to woman, yes, that's true, and bimbos getting their brains blown to bits is not politically correct, and from a strictly aesthetic point of view it's an atrociously bad film, and the only reason its on, along with 50 more like it, is because it's Halloween, and mayhem has taken over for monsters. No longer fun. No longer interesting, given our daily dose of Dahmers and the OJ's. This is just blood and guts, blood and tits, and as I said the tits are fun. But enough about that what about me? Did the computer thing at the bar. Went well. I vacillate back and forth about the merits of any of this writing. You just reread my little missive on the mayhem movies to know a lot of what I have to say is just crap. *Psycho Cop* just ended, by the way and there were actually a few clever moments there, or maybe I'm really full of shit Anyway I got through the reading and then dinner with Bob and Dixie, and their friend Karen, a real cutie, and a neighbor too. You'd think I'd sleep after being so wiped out by the day but no. Pain in the head. Pain in the neck and shoulders. A burning in my left shoulder. But I'm still fucking awake. And I'm sick of writing crap. The more I take this stuff seriously the worse it starts to sound. I must continue to repeat to myself: *It's only a journal... it's only a journal.*

10/29/95 Another 5 in the morning ditty. Been asleep most of the night since nine o clock. I'm keeping old geezer hours. Sheree went to the NIN concert and party with Skip as my stand in and her escort, thanks to me. Sheree just got back and now I'm awake (for awhile) as she slumbers on. She had a great time but I would have surely hated it. Hours of waiting. Loud music that I don't care that much about. Video and special effects and performances that are rip-offs of me and my earlier days. Sheree was ranting and raving about how they ripped us off with their multi-video and SM/ piercing performance. I tell her let the complaints stay here. Don't let anyone else hear her ranting this way because it sounds ludicrous and self aggrandizing, even if is true. The piercing thing is still a fad, something we did in performance 10 years ago and have moved on from and out of ever since. Those guys, Bud and Derk and the rest, when they begin to truly lose the hair on their bald heads that they now shave, and the piercing fad has long faded, what will they have left but a bunch of holes? I would have hated the concert, the scene, and the party, even in my healthier days. But now, when I have been feeling like shit and being sick as a perfect excuse, I have yet to be proven wrong in making the choice to stay home, wheher it be from a party, a concert, or dinner with geeks. Home is where the Bob is. There is nothing out there that I need or want anymore. I have filled my life, and my holes, with "Geezer Vision." I'm in my ruminating phase. I'm opting at every turn to stay home, wheeze, complain, and go to bed early. Why if I didn't have only a year to live I'd kill myself.

10/31/95 Halloween. Happy anniversary for Boo and Scary. And we are happy in spite of the sad times we have to deal with. Fifteen years ago she opened the door at Alexandra's house in the Palisades and she was greeted by me, made up to look like a dead guy. My date at the time, Karen, was hot and sexy but dumb and boring and reeking of cigarette smoke. Not for me. Not for long. 15 years later, Karen's dead, Alexandra's dead, and I'm the dying guy for real, no-make up necessessary. And no energy either. And my head's not screwed on straight because this isn't the 31st. It's late at night on the 30th. Tomorrow's our anniversary. Now to be really confusing, it was really yesterday. I'm just filling in the gaps to finish off this last entry for October where I fell asleep while trying to write and woke up and went on about life. So the 15th anniversary's over. It passed without incident. Dinner with Kirby and Rita. Home and lots of sleep. Not much art. Question is, will there be a sixteenth anniversary, or will she have to dig me up?

11/1/95 Pain and nausea. Muscle aches in my neck, my shoulders and my lower back. Short of breath when I going from point a to point b. So what's the point? Headaches as usual. Thought they were gone for awhile this afternoon, but there it is. My head pumped up and my eyes are bulging out and face turning red like somebody's blowing me up with a tire pump. Seems to get worse the more short of breath I am. OK, I'll try the bipap again tonight. Skip and his friend, Erin, the woman who works for the PR firm for NIN. Tiny little thing with shocking violet hair, a waist as wide as my head, which would fit fine right between her pencil thin thighs once those painted on leather pants were unzipped and split down the middle. But she was taken and so am I. Just a 15 year itch and the fantasies of an old man. Another young nubile looking longingly at the great and masochistic, once and future BOB. Damn this headache hurts.

11/2/95 In a non-writing, non-caring phase with this journal. Hard to believe I'm two months away from an entire year of writing with only a few days missed here and there. But when the heroes are as boring as this, why bother. Discipline. The rules. Being a good boy. That's why. Question is, what will the next journal be like and how long will it last? I go through phases where I think it won't be long at all. Every muscle in my torso hurts. Every breathing muscle, from my lower rib cage up to my neck and shoulders. And don't forget the headaches. Let me take a break in these complaints while I pee… I'm back, out of breath, head pounding, but the bladder's better. I told you this shit was boring. Sheree's been acting goofy lately. Menopause. Hot flashes. Freaking out. Obsessing on the smallest things. Partly menopause, partly her UCI show and the usual shit she puts herself through when before an opening, expecting me to do all the work, when she knows I can't, looking for some magic computer program that will do all the artsy fartsies in a couple of key strokes without her having to spend any time learning the computer, like she'd like to have an editing machine that will edit her video's without her having to watch the damned things before or after. That was my job. I was that machine. But time is shorter now and besides, I won't always be here, so if she wants it done she has to either get into it herself or give it up. She keeps saying she's going to give it all up when I die, which is ironic since I wouldn't gotten involved in all this art crap if it weren't for her. I would have spent all my time as her slave, writing dopey little ditties in the back room. Would I have lived as long? Would we have stayed together? Would life have been so good? Probably not.

11/3/95 hey mark:

i'm typing to the tune of leonard cohen. it's 3 am and *McCabe and Mrs. Miller* is on tv. as always sheree and i are still tv junkies and the box stays on throughout the night sifting in and out of our dreams. once i woke up and my heart started beating fast cause i saw two guys fighting outside our bedroom window and one of them stabbed the other one. i was really scared until i realized it was some old movie on tv reflected in the glass. but leonard and altman are a nice reflection as i write to mark in the north country.

sheree says hi. she's awake too. we do this all night: sleep, wake, sleep, wake, etc. she has an anti-snoring band-aid on her nose, and i do declare i think it's working. maybe i can take out these damn earplugs. obviously there's lots to catch up on and lots to talk about, and obviously i'm not doing such a remarkable job of it but e-mail will make it so much easier in the future to keep abreast of things and stay in touch.

that's it for now. back to leonard. back to sleep. back to killers in the window. love to you and jackie, and andrew and the mutt.

love bob and sheree

bfsm and fstoprose

ps

i'm enclosing the file *pain journal* which is an edited and cleaned up version of this year's ongoing journal that i gave to somebody for an anthology called *when pain strikes*. i've been keeping this little journal since january, at least a paragraph a day, getting much more serious about it when the laptop arrived. forcing myself to get something together for this anthology i suddenly looked back and was shocked to see that i actually had some writing that i was proud of. so here goes. there's much more where this came from, some good, some awful. enjoy.

11/4/95 Riker accidentally doubled my Dilaudid prescription, so I'm "accidentally" swallowing double so maybe I can "accidentally" get a buzz as well as dull this all-encompassing pain I've been feeling, from my head to my toes and all points in between. I'm sick of being Mr. Good Patient. Gimmie drugs. All I've done today is moan and complain and try to move from point a to point b. Sleep at night is on and off and very weird. Once again it's 5 am right now and I've been up for a couple of hours after waking with a pounding head after coming to bed around 10. Bad news day. First, this morning out of the blue I start thinking about the Halloween that first Halloween party and the fact that now, fifteen years later, Karen's dead and Alexandra's dead, and I was wondering who else was dead, when, ironically, I'm sitting here still alive, barely, and say to Sheree, "I wonder if Scott's still alive?" Literally 30 minutes later the phone rings and it's

Deborah, boring Deborah, Scott's ex-Deborah. Scott's dying of liver failure. He may be dead already for all we know. I should have tried to call the hospital today but I got absorbed in my own daily impending death. Am I just a cold bastard, totally self-absorbed, or so familiar with death by now that it no longer has any effect on me? *Sleepless in Seattle* is on the dumb tv. More death. It starts with Tom Hanks' wife dying. It moves me more than the news about Scott, or even the other awful news today: the assassination of Itzak Rabin. Cause I'm not thinking about the death itself, but Sheree's survival afterwards and my parents unending sadness that makes me want to cry. Dying is a piece of cake — no, dying is hard — death is a piece of cake for the dead. It's the surviving spouses, families and nations who suffer the most, having to mourn day in and day out for the rest of *their* lives, while we dead folk are resting six feet under, not a care in the world, fucking selfish sons of bitches that we are.

11/7/95 As I type this into the laptop here in bed at 2 am Sheree's massaging my neck and back muscles with that penis thing, that wooden massager, the stick with two balls on it, two bright and shiny wooden balls that roll across my neck and vertebrae like a mini-steam roller doing its damnedest to flatten the pain and smooth the kinks in this deadened strip of pavement I call my life. But the pain has been overwhelming lately. That's why I've missed a few days here in the journal. The pain has been more than just headache pain. Last Thursday I started getting this pain in my lower back on the right side. Now it's become a stabbing pain every time I change position or inhale. This morning, just trying to get dressed, the pain was so bad my teeth were chattering. So what does Riker say? Nothing. He never says anything. What's there to say? He took an x-ray, which he hasn't seen yet, so maybe tomorrow it will turn out to be something tangible that we can put our fingers on and do something about, but I'm not holding my breath. He did give me a new prescription for a new non-narcotic (of course) pain killer that's supposed to work on the endorphins and block the sensation of pain. Uh huh. It may have quelled the pain somewhat. I was able to forget the pain a while and futz around with the computer and drag my ass to Debbie's, but at Debbie's we had to cut it short because I was screaming in agony every time I tried to cough or take a breath. I came home in a real foul mood. Sheree was stoned, which didn't help matters. But she was as loving as always, which did help matters. She's asleep now. No more massaging. No more penis thing. Speaking of penis thing, in the midst of all this suffering and complaining, the real penis thing has had a little more life in it lately. I wrote about the masturbation last week when Rita called. But I forgot to mention the spontaneous fuck we had on the living room couch. I think it was Thursday or Friday. I know it was shortly after our anniversary because I was thinking wow what a nice anniversary present. There's life in the old goy yet. But not tonight, dear, I've got a headache.

11/8/95 It's just more complaining. That's what the day is. That's what the writing is. Tonight it's nausea and a stomach that's twisted in knots. Constipation too. And no appetite what so ever. Could this be connected to the chest pain, the stabbing pain when I inhale, the lower back pain? Maybe a bowel obstruction putting pressure on the diaphragm? Could such a thing happen? Do I even know what the hell I'm talking about? That's the problem, I don't. It's the doctors who are supposed to make the diagnosis. But weeks go by and the list of complaints just grows longer and I don't think anyone's taking me seriously enough. There's so much more I'd rather be doing than talking about this shit all the time. I canceled the trip to Shiffler's place in Greenville, Ohio. It was hard convincing Sheree that it's just torture for me to go on these trips, especially when there's no real reason for me be there other than as an observer. It's too much work. Getting off the couch is too much work. I feel guilty as hell about it, like I used to feel when I stayed home sick from school. I'd spend the whole day, or the whole week sometimes, wondering how sick am I really? Am I exaggerating or pretending? I'm still driving myself crazy. But I'm dying aren't I? I'm in pain aren't I? The problem is, I set it up so that pain was supposed to be good, something to endure and to conquer. Anything short of that feels like failure. Most of the time I know this is all bullshit thinking but I have to own up to it because it is there and it does make me nuts sometimes.

11/9/95 Can't do it. Pain's subsided but I'm exhausted. Falling asleep. Can't write. Wrote long e-mail to Mark and Jackie earlier today, but no more, not tonight. Kirby and Rita just left after renting a laser for us to watch. *Amadeus.* I objected. Can't stand Tom Hulse and I can't stand all that music. The next film was some cops and robbers and surfers thing with Keanu Reeves and Gary Busby. Stupid, but it held our attention. At least we didn't have to look at that asshole Tom Hulse and listen to that music. Gotta sleep now. Sheree's upstairs engrossed in another jigsaw puzzle. Have to drive her to the airport early in the morning. I bowed out of Ohio, but she's still going. Why oh why Ohio? 'Cause it'll be fun. The only fun I want right now is sitting on the couch or lying flat on my back in this bed. That's it.

11/10/95 I hate to be so monotonous but I'm still in awful pain. Now the left side's killing me when I inhale. I literally slept all day on the couch. My stomach's hurting, my chest is hurting, and I can't get anybody to do any think about it. Sometimes I think they're missing something and I'm going to die earlier than I have to before they catch it. The worst of it is the waste of time. Days like this filled with nothingness are horrible. I don't even want to write this crap but I'm forcing myself to. But not for long. Sheree's in Greenville. Drunk as a skunk last time she called. But she's having fun, and I'm glad I'm home, dull as a skull. In bed. Suffering. Dying.

11/11/95 Open my eyes. Rouse myself. Drag my hands onto the keys and try to tap into something in my brain besides complaining, but there's not much else there. Even straight reportage would be a recitation of pain and more pain. I woke up this morning from a dream that I was in so much pain that I was late for Dr.

Obler. I wanted to cancel my appointment because I was feeling so bad, but it was too late and I felt guilty about it so I was trying to drag my ass out of the house to get over there and then I woke up with one of the worst headaches ever, like nails in my eyes. And chest pains and rib aches. I didn't know how I was going to get out of bed or how I was going to get upstairs. By the time Debbie called at 10 am I was in near tears. Finally I took two Percocet and two Dilaudid and that dulled everything enough that I could get upstairs. But I didn't do shit all day. I'm beginning to think what kind of life is this. Fuck the pain relief. I want morphine to make me happy long enough to get some goddamned work done while I still have time to do it. What's the use of hanging on day after day whining and complaining and sleeping on the couch from sunrise to sunset, freaking out at the thought of anything more strenuous than groping toward the bathroom to take a shit. I'm extremely depressed about all this. Every week I go to see Riker and every week he says I look fine, sound clear, and my x-rays are unchanged. But day after day goes by like this. If it's just the cf and there's nothing they can do about the way I feel than why don't they give me the kind of drugs that will let me forget about the shit long enough to get something done. Otherwise I might as well die right now and forget about it.

11/12/95 Physically not so bad today, thanks to my self-prescribed double dosage of Percocet and Dilaudid throughout the night. I still get knife-like pains in the back while trying to take in deep breaths at Debbie's. Arthritis perhaps from all the wear and tear from coughing my fool head off. I' m literally coughing my joints apart. Like some sort of weird Mr. Destructo wind-up toy, my body is exploding in ultra slow motion. KABLOOEY! Only problem is it hurts like mother fucking hell. Pain pain pain. Odd that what was once the fuel that ignited my soul has become the very thing that dampens my spirit. It just ain't fun no more. And for christsake it's all I talk about isn't it? Speaking of Christ and talk and pain, I made my bible thumping, dimwitted, self-centered, clueless brother John, John the Baptist, who might as well be walking around with his head cut off, for all the good it does him (or anyone else), I made the crybaby cry, and now I feel bad about it. I sat around here all day on God's day of rest after a miserable weekend of pain and discomfort and thought instead of wondering why John hasn't called me or Mom in months (he says it's been a month, but I say months, with an "s" for "stupid": month or months, what difference does it make: where the fuck is he again?) His feelings are hurt cause no one called him on his birthday. But where's he been? What kind of bible does he read? I tell him Mom is going to go through an awful time of it when I die, worse than with Tish. He wants to know why I think that. He wants me to tell him why I think Mom is going to go through such hell when she loses me. It's like Lenny asking George about the fucking rabbits! It's like some dumb kid asking Daddy to tell him why the sky is blue. Well I'm sick of John, father of 4, acting like a fucking dumb kid all the time. If he wants to know why people don't call him on his fucking birthday he should grow up and pick up the phone like a man and ask somebody why. Put himself on the line to take some heat. But I found out, when the heat gets too high, he just breaks down and cries and you have to feel sorry for the stupid bastard, even if you're the one who's dying. Even if you're the one who spends the weekend in constant pain. He finally asks what kind of pain I'm having and I tell him about the shortness of breath with the slightest activity, the knife in my ribs, the pounding in my head. That's when the waterworks start. That's when I say I'm sorry baby brother, I didn't mean to call you and beat up on you or anything. I just wanted to give you a brotherly wake up call to remind you that, aside from the fact that I'm dying, you've got a mother who just might need the comfort of her son in her hour of need, and if you don't do something about it now, you're going to lose her forever, never mind me, you idiot. What bible are you reading from? What happened to turn the other cheek and honor thy mother and father? As usual he says he's glad I called, yeah, yeah yeah. But the more I think about it, the more it burns me up. Thought about it all the way to the airport to pick up Sheree. And I still couldn't get it out of my head even though I was glad to see her. But she's home now and it's late at night and there's some movie on tv about alien abductions and I just got done calling my brother John a bunch of names on the computer, so all's right with the world. Thank you, Jesus.

11/13/95 2 a.m. Took a bath tonight and fell asleep but woke up dreaming of awful pain in my lower back and what do you know the dream came true. Now that I'm awake I should at least update the journal. If a journal is supposed to be an ongoing account of one's day to day activities or accomplishments, if not just interesting thoughts and ruminations, what the hell is this stuff I've been writing lately where the most that ever changes is the channel on the tv. Occasionally I turn an interesting phrase and I can be cute and I can make the audience weep over my sad predicament or laugh in spite of themselves at my sardonic wit. But sometimes a journal is just a journal and mine is folding in on itself with all the dullness and the redundancies of camping out on death's door. And today's entry is: Dear Diary: Canceled Obler today because I had such awful rib pain and shortness of breath while trying to get ready to leave the house I had to quit at the last minute. So I stayed naked all day and I can't tell you what else I did because it's not worth the cyberspace it's written on. The bath was the big event. And now this late night stupid ass movie about valley heavy metal stoners, but hey, it had some nice tits in it so it wasn't a total loss. The only bug in my butt now is I wonder if I should have e-mailed my mother the journal entry about John? Not sure if she'd get the humor. Not sure if it even has humor.

11/14/95 Another 5 a.m.-er after waking up gasping — oops: no oxygen. Must have ripped it off during the night, but there it is. I stick it back up my nose and, voila! I'm breathing again, if that's what you call it. Still in pain but not as bad, thanks to dou-ble scoops of P and D. Kirby drove me down to the CF clinic. All signs point to gallstones. Going down for an ultra sound tomor-row. Leaving no stone unturned. God, this journal has degenerated into nothing but reportage. I've got gallstones. Film at eleven. After my phone call to John the other day he apparently decided to honor his mother after all — with a surprise visit. And that's where he is now. And he's talking about coming our way next. I'm glad our little talk got his ass in gear but him down shifting over here just yet? With Sheree's UCI show, and my gallstones, or whatever the hell it is, I can't deal with much of anything else. And I can't deal with this news reporting any more either. I'm falling asleep. jjjjjjjjjjjjjjjjjjjjjjjjjjjjjjjj See?

11/16/95 I fall asleep but a dream of searing pain ripping across my insides wakes me up and I'm crying out for real because it is real, and I'm wondering if I'm going to have to be brought into the emergency room, just how bad is this? What are we missing? It's not gallstones. I was so exhausted yesterday, inching my way down the hospital corridor, hunched over in the elevator up to the expectant mother's waiting room, waiting for my ultra sound. But I ain't giving birth to nothing but shit. Nothing wrong with my gallbladder. All they find is that my kidneys are slightly enlarged. Compared to what? So it's back hobbling through another hospital for a blood test and a urinalysis. So by the end of the day I was too wiped out to write. Too wiped out again tonight even though I didn't go anywhere. But my wayward brother John did show up here. I felt like Michael Corleone accepting Fredo back into the family. John didn't have much to say, and he didn't stay long, but he had to come by to pay his respects to his brother to get back in the family's good graces. Johnny, you broke my heart. Maybe I should have done more or said more than show video's of camp and talk so much about myself, but what else do I have. So he's going through a major life crisis like the rest of us did and do and will always go through. Sheree comes home from school, loving me to pieces and telling me how she wants to grow old together, how she wants to watch me become a crochety old man, how she couldn't live with anyone but me after I'm dead. This breaks my heart more than anything, the pain I'm putting her through, and the pain she's going to feel when I'm gone. I can joke about it and joke about it, and I can say I'm ready for it, but I can't stand what it's doing to my family and Sheree. I want to grow old with her too. She already has a crochety old man, it's just too bad we can't have the years to go along with it.

11/17/95 Woke up again at 2:30 last night dreaming of a hot friction like internal pain. It's frightening, like something from *Alien* is going to come ripping through my "tummy" (as they say in pediatrics). Since I was up I started watching a film about autopsies. Torsos, maggots, bullet holes and a bag of bones with two jellyfish-like things which turned out to be the remains of a woman and her breast implants. Hard time sleeping after that, not because of that, just can't sleep lately. And I can't eat either. I did finally take an Oxazepam at 6 am and I slept till 12, but I woke up all stiff and groggy and hurting like hell. And I had this yucky dream whereby dad and I were going to have sex together. We're both naked and he asks me where the lubricant is and I kind of half heartedly point to some baby lotion in the bathroom. "Baby lotion won't do for me," he says. "Don't you have anything else? I'm proud of the fact that I've always been sexually adventuous, but I'm thinking to myself that this is really over the line. But I can't lie to my dad and tell him where the good lubricant is and he start slathering it all over his hairy chest. I don't think in real life my dad even has a hairy chest, but he's slathering away and it's getting all over me in big thick goopey globs. I look around and see that there's no towel to wipe off with after we're done, and then it hits me: after we're done with what? I finally tell him that this is way too much for me… exhausted, more later…

11/18/95 Awake. Tired. Irritable. Annoyed that it's midnight and Sheree has the nerve to sleep while I'm up watching the unfunny *Saturday Night Live* with a wheezing in my chest that won't stop and a pain in my left side that won't stop, and a pounding in my head that won't stop. The complaints just don't stop… but I stopped. The pain was so unbearable I had to stop writing, put

the bipap on to see if it would help me breathe, and then try to get some sleep. Now here I am 6 hours later after waking up in agony, drooling all over my pillow, gasping for air. After doubling and tripling my Dilaudid and Percocet I finally feel pleasantly groggy. That's all I want is to feel pleasantly groggy so I can focus on my work or get a good night's sleep or whatever the hell else I want to do that doesn't involve clenching one part of my body or another and screaming. Now I'm dozing, and that's ok. Spent all day yesterday fighting with Microsoft Word's Print Merge trying to print labels for Sheree's UCI postcards. Her thesis show is a week from Tuesday. Naturally she's anxious about it and is dependent on my help, but I'm trying to wean her away from me doing a whole hell of a lot, at least physically, because physically, there's very little I can do. I did finally get a grasp on the label thing so most of those are done. And I'm just about finished editing the video tape for her. All this needs to be done this weekend in preparation for the possibility that I may once again wind up in the hospital. — suddenly sle;k gpp\\\\\\\\
\\
\\
\\
\\
\\
\\
\\
\\
\\
\\
\\
\\
\\
\\
\\

11/19/95 All those slash marks last night are from my sleeping fingers. I finally did get to sleep thanks to drugs. But I woke up with the same screaming and moaning about the same pain in the lower left side. What kind of pain travels around like this? Now it's in my middle left chest and my neck is stiff on the left side. I also woke up with bruised eyelids, especially the right eye. It looks like somebody punched me in the eye. And to the malaise a fever of 100.5. A long day of printing Sheree's UCI mailing labels and editing her chicken soup tape, and then my drug soup of two Percocet and two Dilaudid and I can't bear to write another boring word. Gotta go before the slash marks get me.

11/21/95 Cold in here. "In here" being the hospital again. Don't have to explain why. This journal has deteriorated into a redundant catalogue of complaints. Most of the time I feel so lousy all I can do is give a rundown of how lowdown I am and that's it. Lately I've been skipping the writing all together. I miss the paragraphs that had that sparkle and transcended the personal day to day reportage. But when the sparkle isn't there, this is, after all, a journal, my private diary, something to reflect upon years from now when I'm old and gray… yeah, sure. Even now I came up with a semi-clever exit line to get out of this entry even though it was a very busy day, feeling awful and helping and trying to finish some computer stuff for her UCI show and get myself ready for the hospital. There's lots of pain issues to discuss. But I don't want to go into any of it. I have a backache and a headache and I want to stop writing, plug in my phone line and check my e-mail before checking out for the day. Actually I've been real groggy and out of it all night, thanks to a little itty bitty mistake made by the nurse. She asked me if I wanted something for pain and I said yeah, sure, even though the pain was somewhat subdued at the time. I could hear her outside my door getting my meds ready and it sounded like she was preparing for an IV of some sort. I'm like a cat who perks up at the sound of the can opener. Tuna? Demerol? That's funny, cause Riker said he wouldn't give me that yet. I thought I was getting Dilaudid. It is Dilaudid but it's IV Dilaudid. I figured Riker was trying something new. What a weird feeling. Like being kicked in the head by a horse. Not the rush like Demerol. More like a drop. And I stayed that way for several hours. Turned out that there was a misunderstanding in the orders, so no more of that. And no more of this.

11/22/95 Missing, and now probably dead model on tv. The press is just itching for another real life murder extraviganza. More OJ. It's sweeps month. Over-hyped Beatles, night after night. New "reunion" songs that should have stayed in the dusty drawers they came from. What a hardass I am. I've got a compression fracture of the 8th vertebrae, most likely a result of years of steroids and all the coughing. That's what I find out after a day of bone scans and x-rays. Don't know if there's anything to do about it but at least we know what it is now and I've got their attention. I'm finally getting Demerol. I tried morphine but I didn't like it. It made me nauseous and it didn't have that sweet relief that Demerol did. If Demerol is a slice of orange, then morphine is a lemon.

11/23/95 I don't know if it's the hospital, the Demerol, Thankgiving or the Beatles Anthology on tv, but I feel depressed. Waves of depression. I'm asking for the Demerol every two hours, but I don't know what I'm feeling in between. I've spent so many months feeling like shit that now it's almost a habit. Writing is definitely not a habit now. I have to force myself to write this just to keep the journal up to date, but there's nothing in my brain, nothing I can filter down through my fingers and into the computer. That makes me sad. I'm pretty scrambled up there in thee brain. I fell asleep this and the nurse woke me up around 5:30 pm I had no idea where I was or what time it was. I thought it was 5:30 in the morning. I don't think I've screwed my head on straight since then. And to make matters worse, the Beatles are breaking up. How can I go on?

11/24/95 I asked them to try me out on the PCA pump (patient controlled access) to see if I'd get better Demerol coverage with less of the drug. I hate this nausea and weird oder in my nose and strange taste in my mouth, and this gloom and doom feeling I have. Sometimes I watch things on tv and it makes me anxious. Everything suddenly seems evil and ugly. I saw parts of *The Seven Year Itch* today and it was creepy. Marilyn Monroe was garish-looking and frightning. My nerves are shot. So I thought the PCA would make things smoother, and maybe it would have but I didn't get PCA but I got a constant drip of Demerol. It seemed fine at first but I lost the pleasure of the initial spurt of juice. Sure it didn't last too long, but now it was gone completely. Not so with the pain. After a while it was back in full force and I seemed even more nauseous and jittery than before. So I'm back to having the nurses give me a push every two hours. That's another thing I missed. I looked forward to the nurses coming in every couple of hours with their syringes to blow this pain away.

11/25/95 The pain saga continues. I didn't like the pump so I went back to having them shoot me up every two hours. There's no perfect solution. I never get quite enough coverage. The pain in my back goes away for awhile, but then it comes back. I'm uncomfortable most of the time, or I'm jittery and anxious from the drug, nauseous and I have no appetite, losing weight instead of gaining the way I usually do, but I can't eat. Ain't this fun?

11/26/95 One month away from my birthday. I should live so long. Live long and perspire. Drenched in sweat after each Demerol, and then the sweat goes away and the pain comes back. Along with it I have this strange drug-induced depression, like I'm halucinating a depression. I'm worried about everything. I asked for an anti-anxiety pill last night, but instead of reducing my anxiety it knocked me out and freaked me out because I thought I might not be able to wake up. So now anti-anxiety pills are making me anxious. And this writing sucks so why bother?

11/28/95 I didn't write anything because I was in pain or I was on drugs or having such an anxiety attack I couldn't use my fingers anymore. Head kills me while I wait for dem dem dem Demerol. Just saw another pain doctor, second one today. Yes we're going for the home IV pain pump. Feel like a fool. Why do I feel, now that I'm getting what I asked for, that I didn't really need it in the first place? That I was exaggerating just to get the drugs. Moronically guilty. Sheree's show tonight. I'm escaping to see Sheree's show.

November Med Complaints

11/1/95 Pain and nausea. Muscle aches in my neck, my my shoulders and my lower back. Short of breath... Headaches as usual. My head pumped up and my eyes are bulging out and face turning red like somebody's blowing me up with a tire pump. Seems to get worse the more short of breath I am.

11/2/95 Every muscle in my torso hurts. Every breathing muscle, from my lower rib cage up to my neck and shoulders. And don't forget the headaches.

11/4/95 Sleep at night is on and off and very weird. Once again it's 5 am right now and I've been up for a couple of hours after waking with a pounding head after coming to bed around 10.

11/7/95 But the pain has been overwhelming lately. That's why I've missed a few days here in the journal. The pain has been more than just headache pain. Last Thursday I started geting this pain in my lower back on the right side. Now it's become a stabbing pain everytime I change position or inhale. This morning, just trying to get dressed, the pain was so bad my teeth were chattering. Riker gave me a new prescription for a new nonnarcotic pain killer that's supposed to work on the endorphins and block the sensation of pain. It may have quelled the pain somewhat. I was able to forget the pain a while and futz around with the computer and go to Debbie's, but at Debbie's we had to cut it short because I was screaming in agony evrery time I had to cough or take a deep breath.

DECEMBER 1995

12/2/95 I haven't written in the journal… wait, what's today's date? Today's date is December 2, 1995. I haven't written in the journal since the last time I wrote in the journal because I'm in the hospital, of course, but I mean, I've been in pretty bad shape. IN PAIN. They finally believe me, that I'm in pain when I practically passed out in front of them this time. OW! There's another left over vestige of it, a little crap in my right side, spasm in my right side. And I'm on liquid, I'm on IV Dilaudid. Yea! Now I have this new toy since I can't get to the computer, this little digital recorder which sound-wise isn't much better than the lousy little, tiny tape recorders but it's supposed to be much better… sons of bitches… why? It doesn't sound very good In the meantime this is what I'm working worth. You get it?

So where the hell have I been? So where the hell am I? I've been in hell, and I'm still in the hospital. Since the last entry (Sheree's opening, which was a great success, but very difficult for me, hard to talk to people, shooting pains when I tried to talk, not doing well at all… but I was there), I was the walking dead trying to make it from the elevator, even with Scott W.'s help. Tasco, my nurse, was shocked at how I looked and I was shocked at how I felt — like shit, like all the shit I felt in the previous six weeks rolled into one, and later that night it got to be a hundred times worse. The Demerol was just a bad taste in my mouth and crazy juice in my head. Everything I thought of seemed like it was going to fall apart or get ripped apart at any moment. Every four hours I waited for my shot of Demerol but there was no buzz and the pain never quit. If I laid on my right side it calmed down a while and I started to fall asleep, but then it just crept over to the left side and I woke up screaming all over again. Finally, they gave me an antianxiety pill/ muscle relaxant called Atavan, and I slept for almost two days — that's where the hell I've been. We've also switched from Demerol to IV Dilaudid with a PCA pump: *beep beep, beep beep* YEAH!

12/3/95 Hard to believe it's winding down — the year, the journal, my life. Still screaming out in pain today. My right lower back has a huge throbbing muscle like a twisted yam. It's been better for the past couple of hours, thanks to Clonopan, another muscle relaxant, another sleeper, too, although here I am still awake. Have to keep at the journal. Have to get back to my work. Stop the complaints, but there's so much to complain about and nothing to write about because nothing happens anymore but medical torture. One bit of bad news: Scott (Jim Scott) died today. Already a month ago we were almost surprised to hear that he was still alive but very sick and still we never called. I tried calling the hospital but I kept getting a recording, and I meant to keep trying but I guess I had my own distractions from the grim reaper.

12/6/95 Where do the days disappear to? Drug stew. I blabbed some informative nonsense into the recorder but now (3 am) is not the time to transcribe it, even though I've got to transcribe it soon since I think I've used up the entire 36 minutes of digital space for my dull meanderings. So why am I awake here in my lovely hospital bed, the sounds of *Perry Mason* squeaking through my little bedrail command post, right next to the up/down controls and the red nurse's head icon which is supposed to summon a friendly comforting nurse to help me through the night to soothe my pain or aid in my comfort, but I don't dare press the symbolic Nightingale because it will only summon the 200 pound Dorothy who "needs this tonight like she needs a hole in the head." I was sound asleep but woke up as usual with a pounding head and a nasty itchy coughing attack, tears running down my cheeks and face all red and puffy. I put my nurse's light on and Dorothy appeared with my night time antibiotic, nasty as hell. I asked for Viciodin and Clonopen for my head and back. "I only got two hands," is what I get. I'm already feeling vulnerable cause I went to sleep with a stupid conversation with Sheree about how much time I spend in the hospital away from her like it was my choice. I'd been in a bad mood already. I'd been depressed already, even though I'm supposedly getting better — I even took a walk around the halls today — but I'm depressed about the whole process of dying, feeling sorry for myself, pissed at the world, pissed at Michael Jackson, whom the press is fawning over because he passes out while rehearsing with Marcel Marceau. He has an IV! He has oxygen! He's just too fucking stupid to drink some water while he's rehearsing so he fainted. Asshole! So I was ranting to Sheree, slightly pissed that she didn't come down to see me, but not begging the issue. But she keeps pushing this hospital or her routine, and that's just not the way it is. I'm here when I have be, and I'm the only one who can make that call, and she just better trust that I know how to take the best care of myself to keep myself around the longest so I *can* be home and doing something worthwhile while I'm there. But tonight Dorothy blows it all by pulling a nurse Ratchet. She gives me my Vicodin and Clonopen and says, "Here, take this one too." I say, "What is it, poison?" But it's only Theopholin. Gulp. "Would you please shut the overhead light?" I ask, ever so gingerly. "When I get to the door, Bob." Great. So when she comes back to adjust the beeping IV pump she turns on the bright overhead light again and leaves. I don't dare ask her again to remember to turn the damn thing off and of course she doesn't, so I sit here at 3 in the morning with the light shining as bright as an operating room, so I read my Tod Browning book. At least there's darkness there, and death to scary oversized freaks.

12/7/95 Bitching all day about many things: the deadly night nurse, Dorothy. "I've only got two hands." If she had three, one of them would be wrapped around my neck or shoved up my ass I'm sure; the Dragnet interrogation team of pain doctors who don't want to give me the IV Dilaudid I need, the stuff that works the best. Joe Friday had more respect for his suspects than these fuckers have for me. After playing good Doc, bad Doc, and grilling me about what pain meds I said worked and what I say doesn't they say ok, IV Dilaudid it is, if that's what it takes. And then they go out into the hall and I can hear them mumbling, and Robin, the cool nurse, comes in and tells me that they asked her, "How well do you know this guy?" Like I'm trying to pull a fast one... tired

12/14/95 Early morning. Home. Sun's not up yet, so I'll still call it the 14th. Been writing a lot lately but not in the journal. Letters. E-mail. Mark and Jackie. Kevanne. Ed Smith. I start out answering their long unanswered inquiries to me and my replies become long winded recaps of my most recent hellish days. It's all the on-going saga of "Bob," even my involvement with friends. No wonder some of them want nothing to do with me. They have their own self-centered sagas and don't need me and my sorry tales to muck it up. But I don't really feel that. They're fucked for not calling, whoever they are. I'm a good friend, even in the midst of making a career of my own personal hell I always call.

12/15/95 Quick end of the day entry cause I'm so exhauasted. Didn't leave the house until 5:00 when Sheree and I went over to the Ford dealership to see if we could turn in the Taurus for a new car but she's still got 5 months left on her lease so it's no go. Shouldn't have copped to being artists. "You're what?" "Artists. We make art." "How much money's in a thing like that?." Uh oh. Forget the car. Jack and his girlfriend Lisa, who is just this much shy of being a bitch. Monica and Dave were here too, so there was lots of yelling and laughing during the X-Files. Felt an air of uptightness eminating from Lisa regarding anti-religious references from Sheree. Just coughed up a wad of blood. That's what I get for laughing bout the lord. Felt better today but still hard to get around with all these fluids infusing into me. I don't think this pump system is the best for my Superior Vena Syndrome. Talking to myself, a la Dilaudid.

12/16/95 End of the day, heading toward the end of the month and the end of the year, and, pretty soon, the millenium, but I don't think I'll get that far. Where I am is in bed with Sheree who is the sick one for a change, with a bad cold (what's a good cold?), that I saw coming a week ago. Lots of thoughts tossing through my head like a drier full of laundry, except when it comes to writing them down all my best thoughts are like mismatched and missing socks. Walking around thinking Dennis Cooper, whom I haven't spoken to in a year, and, except for his reading in New York last year, I haven't seen for about two years. Is he mad at me? Are we fighting? No. It's Dennis to the enth degree. He'd probably answer he phone if I called and say "Bob how are you," and be all embarrassed about not calling and make a bunch of excuses, and say he'd like to get together, but who knows if we ever really will, or if he'll even answer my call, cause he screens all his calls, and if I leave a message he might not even pick up, so maybe I'll fax him. I wrote a long letter to Deborah Drier last October and never heard back from her which makes me think she's done with me too, or else maybe she never got my letter. I wonder why I'm so obsessed with this growing list of people I don't see or talk to anymore? I can't wait to get off the phone when they do call and I can't wait for them to leave when they visit… I think I need to put another quarter in the dryer because I'm just sitting here staring at the television and not writing or thinking anything. I'm starting to feel well enough and lucid enough, when I'm not in the Dilaudid zone, to get some work done. I printed out the entire 1995 journal through October. 75 pages. There were some sparkling moments here and there — good writing I mean — but the latter months seem to have degenerated quite a bit. Too sick. Too distracted. But the journal was intended to be just a day to day record, a minimum of a paragraph a day, and never meant to be read unedited by anyone but me. It was a fluke that so many of the entries became exciting rants and observations that have lead to some good writing. I just hope I can sustain that voice to complete some sort of manuscript. But in the meantime I'm going for a late night dip in the Dilaudid.

In Semi-Sickness and in So Called Health, I'm Still in Love with You

by Sheree Rose

I used to feel sorry for people with physical disabilities because their "affliction" was obvious. They were constantly on display, exposed to the stares and discomfort they provoked in others, becoming unwilling participants in a spectacle they had no control over. We worship beauty and perfection in this culture. Anything less is perceived to be second rate, unworthy of our attention, unless, through circumstances or genes, we are forced to grapple with the beast of our own prejudice and fear. AIDS taught us a terrible lesson: we are all vulnerable to sickness and disease, and we had better learn some new coping mechanisms.

My own awakening began with falling in love with Bob Flanagan in 1980. He was born with a genetic illness, cystic fibrosis, that ultimately killed him. We were together for sixteen years, and I treasure every minute I spent with him.

Bob and I were an unlikely pair. He was twenty-seven when we met; I was ten years older. He was a lapsed Catholic; I was a cultural Jew. He had never been married; I was divorced with two bratty children. He told me that he was submissive man, that he was looking for a woman to serve, to be her love slave, to do her bidding as well as her laundry. Times being what they were, I took him up on his offer.

I treated him like a slave, because that was how he wanted to be treated and besides, I enjoyed having a sexy guy at my beck and call. He told me on our first date that he had a disease called cystic fibrosis, and that was why he had to take a handful of pills with his meal to help with his digestion. I had no idea of the seriousness of his illness until nearly three months later.

I was in a bad mood because Bob was sick with a cold, and we spent our first New Year's Eve together staying home since he didn't feel well enough to go out. As his dominatrix I was furious at having to change my plans and forego a glitzy celebration. As his lover I felt compassion and tenderness—like a mother would for her ailing child. Thus, the beginning of an emotional conflict that would continue for years. I'd made plans to fly up the coast to a friend's wedding on New Year's Day, and Bob encouraged me to go. He felt bad about disappointing me.

It turned out that one of my traveling companions was a registered nurse, and during the course of the afternoon, I told her about Bob, our relationship and his disease. When I said the words "cystic fibrosis" her face visibly blanched. I felt a pang in my heart as she proceeded to tell me just how terrible his condition was, that it wold only get worse and end in premature death, and that I should get out while I still had the chance. Needless to say, I was stunned by her assessment, prognosis and recommendation.

I had come to a turning point, and knew I had to make a choice of whether to commit to Bob and stay with him for the long run, or to cut my losses now before our lives got more enmeshed. I wrestled with this by asking myself questions. Where did our attraction come from? Why did we feel so drawn to each other? Why did we bond so deeply and so soon?

Love is a powerful force. It doesn't respect rules or boundaries. Bob and I fell in love because we felt ourselves to be kindred spirits, outcasts in a society where neither of us fit the norm. His 'sickness' showed, while mine was more hidden. He had strength where I was weak. I encouraged and promoted his creativity. He made me laugh when I was most depressed. I believe Bob's internal quirks were far more elusive than the external evidence of his perverted deeds, once done furtively under the cover of night, and eventually metamorphizing into brilliant public shows at art venues all around the world. Some secrets are carried to the grave. For whatever the reason, what a brave, heroic heart he possessed. We were a totally romantic couple, made larger than life by how we dealt with our imperfections, showing them to the world, incorporating them into our art.

Bob died on January 4, 1996. Between his last entry in The Pain Journal on December 16 and the time of his death, he was in the hospital, in a semi-delirium, too sick to continue the journal.

Not a day has gone by since Bob died that I haven't thought about him, cried about him, lost sleep over him, friends because of him, been frightened without him, lonely without him. I miss the dumb, mundane events that everyone knows who loses someone close to them: watching TV, going shopping, going out to eat, going to the movies, going to bed and falling asleep in each other's arms. I feel frustrated by his permanent absence. I miss the substance of his bones, the semi-smoothness of his lily-white shaved skin. I miss his lightly salty taste and ever-changing facets of his face. *It's Fun To Be Dead* was a song he once wrote. And while it may be for him, it's definitely not true for me. All that remains is a phantom spirit that continues to inhabit, haunt and seduce me.

Recently in Amsterdam, I picked up a man in the Pontaneur Cafe, a converted theater, it still retained an air of theatricality, a place where I could be anyone I wanted, and nobody knew my name. His name was John, a Surinam-born Jew, who had traveled to the United States in the 70's while serving in the Dutch navy. Since the only place he had visited was in Alabama, he had somewhat limited experience with American women, but was eager to enrich his education.

He had been married to an African woman who had come to Holland as a political refugee, but was single now, and looking for someone to keep company with. I told him that I was a widow who had come to Amsterdam to find myself.. We wandered around the neighborhood, he showed me all the cool bars. We drank beer and Geniver, the Dutch version of gin, and held hands as we walked over narrow bridges that spanned the canals. He was very polite and had a pragmatic, down-to-earth view of life which I found very appealing. It was easy to let him take charge; I felt relaxed and cared for, if not very turned on. Later he asked if I wanted to see where he lived, and it was easy to say yes.

Like most apartments in Amsterdam, there were no elevators, and he lived on the fifth floor, so I was a bit breathless and drunk when we finally sat down on the couch. The place was spotless— he told me that cleanliness was an important virtue. He had a wonderful collection of rhythm and blues records. We listened to Marvin Gaye and drank more Geniver.

He asked me if I wanted to have sex with him. He told me he always used "protection," and that we should shower before the act. It seemed so reasonable and matter-of-fact I couldn't think of a reason to say no. When I finished in the bathroom, I followed him into the bedroom, where I lay down on the bed. He took off his towel and I was astonished at the size of his penis, already semi-erect. True to his word, he promptly put on a condom and proceeded to enter me. I viewed this encounter as an experiment in cross-cultural intercourse, and allowed him complete access in the service of closer international relations. It wasn't romantic in the least, but it lasted a long time and it felt like I was doing a good thing, at least on a physical level. When we finished, he said it was time to go to bed, but first we had to shower again. After he closed the bedroom door, he placed a bottle filled with murky liquid on the floor. He said it was another kind of protection, one that would keep any evil spirits away from us while we slept. It seemed reasonable enough, although I realized that I was pretty ignorant of Surinamese-Jewish customs. Actually, I hardly slept at all. I was tossing and turning, and got up to go to the bathroom several times, making sure not to trip over the magical bottle. Finally, I managed to fall asleep sometime before dawn.

When I woke in the morning, John was already up, and making breakfast -strong coffee, scrambled eggs and toast. I told him that I had had a hard time falling asleep. He told me that was due to the fact that the spirit of my dead husband had been just outside the bedroom door, angry that I had spent the night.. He asked me if I had made a pledge to Bob to love him forever. When I answered positively, he said that I had made a mistake and that Bob's spirit was going to haunt me and spoil any chance I would have of being with another man. I was astonished by his interpretation of my restless night, but like everything else he had told me, it made perfect sense. John said that ghosts who are still attached to living people due to prior vows of fidelity watch over their loved ones until 4 a.m. Then they leave while it is still dark. I felt elated that the spirit of Bob was still so close to me and still cared about what I did and who I did it with. I realized that was the cause of my chronic sleeplessness ever since Bob's death. I was comforted by this idea of Bob's continued presence in my life, and I wasn't sorry that we had made vows that were going to last for eternity. Even in death, Bob still influences my life.

That Bob became such an incredibly creative, forthright and funny adult was nothing short of miraculous. Together, we transformed shame and sorrow into a transcendent state that defies logic and reason and death. Bob never gave up; he never showed self-pity; he always looked to the future. And so, until the very end, Bob prevailed.

—Sheree Rose
Los Angeles, 2000

The Complete Smart Art Press Catalogue

Volume I (Nos. 1–10)

Volume II (Nos. 11–20)

Smart Art Press
2525 Michigan Avenue, Building C–1
Santa Monica, California 90404
tel 310–264–4678 fax 310–264–4682
www.smartartpress.com

Printed in the United States
by Baker & Taylor Publisher Services